Seven Stories
WE TELL OURSELVES

A GUIDE TO LIVING CONSCIOUSLY

ANGELA TOMLINSON

Copyright © 2021 by Angela Tomlinson.
All rights reserved. No part of this publication may be reproduced, distributed, or transmitted in any form or by any means, including photocopying, recording, or other electronic or mechanical methods, without the prior written permission of the publisher, except in the case of brief quotations embodied in critical reviews and certain other non-commercial uses permitted by copyright law.

 A catalogue record for this work is available from the National Library of Australia

Tomlinson, Angela (author)
The Seven Stories We Tell Ourselves
ISBN 978-1-922629-08-1

Typeset Sofia Pro Light 10/16
Cover image - Adobe Stock
Cover and book design by
Green Hill Publishing

For my family and friends – you are life.

Contents

Preface vii

Part 1: We tell ourselves stories 1
We all tell ourselves stories 3
We are wired this way 5
There are only seven stories! 7
If we know the seven, we can identify our own stories 8
All of the stories we tell can serve or hinder us 10
We now know the alternatives! 12
Let's make a choice 13
Let's 'Live Consciously' 14

Part 2: The seven stories 19
Overcoming the Monster 23
Rags to riches 31
The quest 37
Comedy 47
Tragedy 57
Rebirth 65
Journey and return 77

Part 3: The stories we tell ourselves 85
Here are our stories 87
Public speaking – everybody's nightmare! 91
Waiting patiently in line... until! 97
Angela goes hard 105
A challenging adventure in a natural wonderland 113
A loving mother 121
Chasing the title of 'best bowler' 129
A suicidal teen 135
Angela jumps out of a perfectly good aeroplane 145

Such a nervous child 151
Living with grief 157
Kelly covets that office 165
Lucy learns to do a 'round-off on the beam' 171
A personal mission 177
Redecorating the house 185
A bully for a boss 191
A beastly husband 199
Sally is the scapegoat 205
A century of problems in the family 213

Part 4: *The Seven Stories We Tell Ourselves* toolbox 221
Using the toolbox: learning to 'live consciously' 223
The power of a growth mindset 227
Identifying the conflict and complications 231
Seeking resolution 237
To serve or to hinder, that is the question 243
Adjusting the telling within the narrative to make it serve you 255
Having conviction in our morals, being 'in the right': the key to
deserving a reward 261
Your superpowers: visualisation and affirmations 271
Journaling 279
Success elixir #1: Box breathing 287
Success elixir #2: Meditation 291
Finding patterns in our narratives 295
The impact of our emotions 305
Hitting on the right narrative 309
Practice, practice, practice 313
The Seven Stories applied: Teaching the monsters 317

Final Words 323
References and Bibliography 329
Acknowledgements 335

Preface

I was fast asleep in the camper trailer, camped on a beach at Ningaloo Station in the far northwest of Western Australia. A deep sleep; a dream sleep. In the dream I had a very clear experience – I was going to write a book. The book was a derivative of the archetypal characters that comes from Jungian psychology. My dream had some very concrete examples of character types and how we might live our lives according to the ideals of these types.

It was October 2020. The craziness of COVID-19 was almost everywhere else in the world. In WA we seemed to be doing really well. We could go on with our lives with a few general health observations, like the new concept of 'physical distancing' which was easily achieved in a state with more than one square kilometre per head of population. A bit of extra hand washing and cleaning of public places and it was all good! Our Premier was determined to keep us safe from the spread of the disease by closing our borders to the rest of the country and the world. If we wanted to travel, we had to travel at home. This meant I could take lots of books and I did. I read a lot! I explored lots of concepts in the self-improvement arena. I explored widely.

I had no conscious idea of Jungian psychology prior to this, so it was in googling archetypes that I made such discoveries. The archetypes, according to the Jungian perspective, are characters that are innate to us. They are a part of our 'collective unconscious' and we live out these characters within ourselves. They appear in our stories. My concept, however, focused more on choosing characters to aspire to. I think this would in some ways contrast to a Jungian perspective unless these characters are very aligned to what is essential to us... anyway, I digress.

I continued reading, watching YouTube videos of thought leaders and exploring my thoughts. I kept a journal of ideas.

Somewhere along the line, I shifted my thinking from archetypal characters to the archetypal narratives. I trained as an English teacher and studied Comparative Literature. I have explored, analysed and taught stories in this frame for over twenty years. An intimate knowledge of stories and story structures is part of my world of work – my thinking patterns – and I have been aware of the idea of archetypal narratives for decades.

I don't know exactly how I decided that this was the concept of my book, but I did find the first entry in my journals where I started to ponder this. I had watched Brene Brown's *A Call to Courage* (2019) on Netflix again! She was describing the time when she was swimming with her husband and he wasn't sharing the same feelings as her, so she was having some negative feelings about it. She talked to him about this and her specific words were, 'The story I am telling myself here...' That was the trigger for this reflection in my journal:

We tell ourselves stories; we make narratives in our mind about our lives in which we are the protagonist. We have 7 archetypal narratives to choose from. You can choose your narrative. There are consequences to the narrative that we tell ourselves. We can choose our narrative actively and therefore have control over our lives, or we can allow ourselves to choose subconsciously and accept the consequences of this.

Interestingly, I did not revisit this journal entry until this book was nearly finished. Even more interesting is that this obviously stayed with me, because this is exactly what I am conveying in this book.

I have been thinking about my ideas, pondering my life and applying this theoretical framework to my lived experience. It makes sense to me, I hope it does to you.

Happy reading, I can't promise it will change your life but I will promise you food for thought. At the very least, I hope this book encourages you to 'live consciously'.

Kindly,
Angela

PART 1

We tell ourselves stories

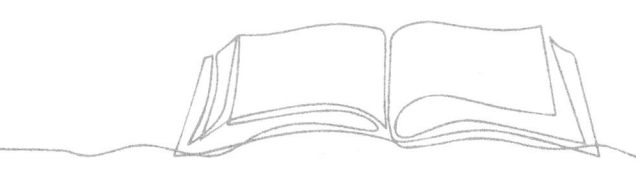

We all tell ourselves stories

Stories are universal, common to every known culture across time. We have stories that have come with humans from the ancients – from the myths of Rome and Greece – through to the current *New York Times* best seller at time of writing, Danielle Steele's *Neighbours*. Story plays a very significant part in human life, and not simply for entertainment. Stories form the basis of communication for us. Telling stories is a way of interpreting the world for ourselves and of sharing our experiences of the world with others.

Christopher Booker's book *The Seven Basic Plots* (2004) is a large tome in which he explains the work he has done in identifying the seven archetypal narratives available to us for telling our stories. He not only explores the seven story archetypes, he talks about the importance of stories to us. According to Booker:

> ...*stories play such a significant role in our lives, as novels or plays, films or operas, comic strips or TV 'soaps'. Through newspapers or television, our news is presented to us in the form of 'stories'. Our history books are largely made up of stories. Even much of our conversation is taken up with recounting events*

> *in everyday life in the form of stories. These structured sequences of imagery are in fact the most natural way we know to describe almost everything which happens in our lives.* **(Booker, p.2)**

Story is significantly important to us. We don't just experience things, we interpret them for ourselves and present our interpretations to others. We regurgitate events and present them in all manner of story forms. And the importance of the practice of storytelling cannot be understated, if we consider the words of Joan Didion:

> *We tell ourselves stories in order to live... We look for the sermon in the suicide, for the social or moral lesson in the murder of five. We interpret what we see, select the most workable of the multiple choices. We live entirely, especially if we are writers, by the imposition of a narrative line upon disparate images, by the 'ideas' with which we have learned to freeze the shifting phantasmagoria which is our actual experience.* **(Joan Didion, The White Album)**

It seems that story telling is a default setting for us, something innate. As Booker says, '...we look at the world in terms of stories all the time. They are the most natural way in which we structure the descriptions of the world around us. Naturally we see our own life as a story...' (Booker, p.573). We interpret our world through story and share our stories with others.

WE ARE WIRED THIS WAY

If all cultures across all of human existence have told stories, then story has to be innate to us, potentially part of how our brain and our thinking are structured. Story seems to be a universal language for us irrespective of our lived experience.

When we look at what story is, we can see that the same rules are in place and recognise this 'truth' for ourselves. And the stories we tell are structured in what is recognisable as 'story'. We don't simply throw words together, we deliberately put them together in ways that are recognisable as this thing we call 'story':

> ...wherever men and women have told stories, all over the world, the stories emerging to their imaginations have tended to take shape in remarkably similar ways. **(Booker, p.3)**

There are rules by which stories are told – there are protagonists and antagonists, there are settings, complications, climax and resolution – and the audience will have strong expectations of these things in the telling of stories. We know instinctively what a story is:

> There is, in fact, no kind of story, however serious or however trivial, which does not ultimately spring from the same source: which is not shaped by the same archetypal rules and spun from the same universal language. **(Booker, p.7)**

We also have expectations of stories when we are exposed to them.

It was Adolf Bastian (1826-1905) who believed the human mind naturally works in certain forms and around certain images, resulting in what he described as elemental ideas that led to the commonality in stories. However, the concepts of elemental motifs, thought structures and essential knowledge we are born with was common amongst the thought leaders of the time and then beyond. Freud saw the unconscious as driving much of human behaviour and in our dream structures he saw archetypal myths, a thought-based experience common to humans. This, for Freud, is limited to sexuality and problems of the individual psyche. Jung took it further and posited that at some deeper psychological level we are all constructed in a very similar way. Jung explored archetypes as a consistent structure across human brains, describing them as 'psychic contents which have not yet been submitted to conscious elaboration and are therefore immediate datum of psychic experience' (Jung, *The Archetypes and the Collective Unconscious* p.5).

Jung also saw stories in the form of fairy tales as naïve and spontaneous products of our souls; and fairy tales and their significance were explored more deeply by his colleague, Marie-Louise Von France. Leap ahead, and this bridged to Christopher Booker's work, which identified consistent story structures that could only boil down to some essence of the human brain or psyche being responsible. This provided an avenue of thought around the consistency of story structures, bringing them very much into consciousness, which became Booker's 30-year journey with *The Seven Basic Plots*. The distillation of narratives over the decades of Booker's work indicates that these structures have a consistency that can only be possible as part of the inherited archetypal structures, described by Jung as the 'collective unconscious'.

THERE ARE ONLY SEVEN STORIES!

It is interesting to observe that we have very limited choices in how stories can be told.

Whilst the work of Joseph Campbell has focused in on the 'monomyth' (the idea that the mythic narratives all boil down to one great story); Christopher Booker has explored human storytelling more extensively, and he found that seven story structures are widely applied. And when I say widely, I mean that all the stories ever told, across time and cultures, even across genres, can be distilled down to seven storylines, so they are all that is available in telling stories.

Don't be disappointed. Our stories are still intriguing, interesting and surprising because the permutations of these structures are potentially infinite! But we can find the seven basic storylines within everything – advertising, movies, history and even the stories we tell ourselves.

When we start to delve into the stories around us we can start to find the commonalities. The storyline that underpins *Beauty and the Beast* is the same as *A Christmas Carol* and *The Lorax*. The story we use to narrate the life of

Barrack Obama is consistent with *Cinderella* and *My Fair Lady*. The challenge of defeating COVID-19 is consistent with *Jaws* and *Jack and the Beanstalk*.

Whilst the details of these stories vary immensely, the threads are remarkably consistent.

IF WE KNOW THE SEVEN, WE CAN IDENTIFY OUR OWN STORIES

Not only are our heads full of stories all of the time; we are each of us acting out our own story throughout our lives. **(Booker, p.701)**

As I have previously established, we tell the stories of our lives to ourselves and in doing so we are consistent with the story structures identified by Christopher Booker. The narratives we use to tell ourselves our stories have a significant impact on how we feel about what is happening in our lives. It absolutely shapes the experience. When we tell ourselves stories and choose to shape our experiences through them we impact the shape of our lives.

Every experience we have that we then think about, mull over, or tell others is narrated to ourselves. And as the narrators of our lives we choose the details and the 'angle' from which to view these experiences. We take the experiences that we are having and interpret them for ourselves – this becomes our reality. When we look at things from a metaphysical stand point, there is the thing we are observing and there is the mind's interpretation. There are the 'facts' and then what we personally attribute to it. There is the experience itself and what we overlay with our imagination. It starts to disturb our sense of things being 'just so' when we dig into metaphysics, but when we start to see this perspective as one with some merit, we can start to see our own thoughts for what they are: interpretations.

Stephen Covey is famous for some very influential books in the self-help genre. In his words: 'The way we see the problem is the problem' (Covey, p.40). And Napoleon Hill, also iconic in this realm: 'You are what you think' (Hill, et al, 1961, p.30). Within this frame, the way we see the story is the story. Humans have long seen things this way – that we are taking what we experience and we are shaping it into a narrative. Additionally, it is worth thinking about the fact that when we narrate stories to ourselves we are either empowered or disempowered in the narrative. We will either feel good about what has happened, indifferent or we will feel bad about it. This is our choice – we get to make it.

When we narrate stories to ourselves we are also choosing our pathway forward because each narrative progresses in a particular way and there are expectations for the pathway to resolution. Therefore, we are also choosing this pathway to resolution. We need to be aware that we can't get away from this particular resolution unless we change the narrative. Of great benefit to us is the clarity we get when we become aware of these storylines. When we are intimately familiar with the seven basic plots and how we are choosing to narrate the story to ourselves, the pathway forward in our lives becomes clearer. We can see what needs to happen.

It pays to be aware of the seven narrative types if we want to be clear about the stories we tell ourselves and we want to understand exactly how we are shaping a problem for ourselves in order to determine what we can do about the issues we are facing. In this way we can understand the story we are telling, know where the story is headed, and know what we need to do to find the resolution we seek within that storyline.

Interestingly, when we take the time to think about how we are telling our stories to ourselves we pull ourselves out of the trauma of being immersed in the narrative. This trauma is the deeply felt emotion of being wrapped up in the events of our lives. Observing the narrative gives ourselves an opportunity to see things impartially from the outside, and to find some clarity over how and what we are thinking. From the perspective of metaphysics we can recognise our thoughts as interpretations, and know that we have choices about how we see the world. These choices impact how we feel and has a domino effect on what we do about things. It pays then, to be active in choosing how we tell our stories to ourselves.

ALL OF THE STORIES WE TELL CAN SERVE OR HINDER US

A good story can entertain, motivate, and teach valuable lessons. That is why it is important we pay attention to the stories we tell ourselves. Sto-

ries can change how we see the world. But they can also impact how we see ourselves – especially if we tell ourselves the same ones over and over again. **(Becker, 2021)**

Each of the narratives has its own pattern for the telling of the story and way of resolving the conflict. Each way of telling our story has pros and cons and, for each story, these can either serve us or hold us back. None of the stories are inherently better than any other, and for each individual, the best choice for each situation can also differ. The pros and cons need to be carefully weighed up and compared in order to determine the narrative that is going to truly serve us in a situation and those that are best left alone.

An interesting study conducted by Kelly McGonigal, a Stanford psychologist, explored stress. She determined that stress itself is not a killer, contrary to popular belief. Plenty of people live with stress without it having adverse health effects. Some people are even energised by stress and work best under stressful circumstances. What McGonigal found, though, was that it is the way in which we talk to ourselves about the experience, how we narrate to ourselves about the source which is driving the stress, that makes all of the difference (Parker, 2015).

When we talk to ourselves in ways that drive our sense of disempowerment, we become trapped in our struggle and our situation becomes untenable. This drives a stress response. When we ruminate on it and continue narrating the story to ourselves in this way we are further disempowered and this is very unhealthy for us.

It pays, then, to choose the narrative that is going to make us feel like we have agency in our lives. To choose the narrative which makes us feel like we have the opportunity to make choices and have a say in how the events progress and will eventually turn out - that we have the power to influence outcomes and have control over our lives.

WE NOW KNOW THE ALTERNATIVES!

If you have ever been involved in a court case, or even watched one on telly, you would see how the same set of facts can be applied to tell a very different story. Likewise, stories can have the same set of events but be narrated in multiple ways.

When we think about our lives, when we talk about our lives, we can tell our stories in many different ways. We can observe the same set of event-based facts and apply them in many of the seven plotlines, if not all. And all are valid. As Stephen Covey points out, 'People can see the same thing, disagree, and yet both be right' (Covey, p.27). Along this vein of thinking, our stories can be told in multiple ways and all of them be true to the facts. What is important is the way in which the events will be perceived emotionally and how we will expect them to play out.

When we are very familiar with the seven plotlines, we can recognise the stories in what we are narrating and see our thinking from the outside. In addition to this, when we are very familiar with all seven we can explore how we feel about the story if we tell it to ourselves in one or more of the OTHER narratives. We are endowed with an opportunity to see things impartially from multiple points of view. We not only know we can tell our stories in multiple ways, we also know *how* we can tell the stories – what our choices are.

LET'S MAKE A CHOICE

Each of the stories has its own way of playing out, its own way of reaching a resolution. Each has circumstances which allow us to determine if they are generally the most appropriate choice for narration or whether they are the least. This is decided by considering the impact they have on us personally and whether they will assist us in achieving our aims.

Being aware of how stories are constructed keeps us focused on the story as a whole and thus, we are forced to consider the outcome of the events and the preferred outcome that we want. We are then, according to Stephen Covey, 'beginning with the end in mind' – one of his seven habits of highly effective people.

If we want to live our best lives, we should choose how we narrate our stories, selecting the narrative that serves us. We can be proactive; an opportunity we have because we are human and we are gifted with this ability.

If we continue to be reflective about our narratives as we live them out, we can also be aware of the moment the narrative no longer serves us and change: 'It is most important to commit yourself to any decision you make and give it all you've got. But if it doesn't work out, change it! Many of us are so invested in making the "right" decision that even if we find we don't like the path we have chosen, we hang in there for dear life... this is the height of craziness' (Jeffers, p.125). Be sure to apply yourself wholeheartedly to seeing your narrative in the way you choose, but do not be afraid to change the narrative when it no longer serves. In order to do this effectively, we just need to be reflecting on our lives, our decisions, our thoughts, our feelings, and making sure we remain in the driver's seat.

LET'S 'LIVE CONSCIOUSLY'

Direct your thoughts, control your emotions, ordain your destiny. **Napoleon Hill and W. Clement Stone.**

Are you living at the whim of your existence, buffeted by winds of change? Are you driven by currents in one direction or another rising and falling at the behest of the tide and crashed upon by the waves of your lived experiences? Or, are you the captain of your ship making the most of opportunities and steering your path, using the weather to your advantage?

If you are taking the helm in your life then you are choosing to 'live consciously'.

Covey suggests that if we don't proactively create our lives and write our own scripts, we will reactively live the scripts handed to us by family, associates, other people's agendas, or training and conditioning. He says we are the creator and that we must take charge of that creation to be a highly effective person (*Seven Habits*, p.100).

It's within our power to tell our stories in our own ways, to choose a narrative that serves us, to be in control of our own lives, and to live consciously.

If we do not live consciously, mindfully approaching our worlds and actively choosing for ourselves, we can be directed by others who want to create habits in us for their own ends. Or we may blindly 'keep doing what we are doing', oblivious as to whether our own habits add value or detract from our lives. Charles Duhigg wrote a fabulous book called *The Power of Habit* (2012). In it he stated, 'One paper published by a Duke University researcher in 2006 found that more than 40% of the actions people perform every day weren't actual decisions, but habits' (p. xvi). This is an appalling reality – we can be so driven by mindless actions that 40% of our lives are based on habit. If that 40% is comprised of inane behaviours such as washing our hair or going to the toilet, this is less of an issue, though I have to say that the mindless approach to the washing up enacted by my children is a source of great consternation for me! However, if we are blindly and habitually going about the big stuff in our lives – what really affects us – we are not living our best lives. We need to make sure we are not falling into habits when we tell our stories to ourselves.

We need to be aware that we are the authors of our own reality, and we need to do this actively and consciously.

Jay Shetty has some expertise in living your best life; he had been a monk for some time and is now applying those practices to a more contemporary lifestyle. In his book *Think Like a Monk* he says, 'We are defined by the narrative that we write for ourselves every day. Is it a story of joy, perseverance, love and kindness, or is it a story of guilt, blame, bitterness, and failure?' (p. 163). When we have choices about our narrative, wouldn't we want to make a conscious choice? The best choice – the choice that has us steering the ship and the choice that gives us the outcomes that we want – the choice that serves us?

Lori Gottlieb is a psychologist who has done some deep reflecting and sharing about the stories we tell about our lives. She urges us to make the best choices we can about how we narrate the stories of our lives to ourselves: 'Life is a process of selecting which stories we listen to, which stories we edit, and which we choose to rewrite. When it comes to the stories of our lives, you should be aiming for your own personal Pulitzer Prize.' I join her in urging you to make the best choice in narrating the stories of your life.

The next part of this book will illustrate for you the seven plotlines so that you can become intimately acquainted with them and be ready to recognise their patterns in the stories you tell yourself. This knowledge will give you the power to live consciously.

PART 2

The Seven Stories

Stories have particular structures. There are some specific expectations that we have around story because, as readers, we innately know these story structures. Christopher Booker has revealed to us in his work that there is one metaplot for all stories.

This begins with the *anticipation stage*. At this point the protagonist/hero experiences the call to adventure. This is followed by a *dream stage* – the adventure begins – the hero has some success and feels undefeatable. Then the frustration stage occurs – the hero confronts the enemy and no longer feels invincible. The *frustration stage* grows into the *nightmare stage* – the climax of the plot – the protagonist/hero feels hope is apparently lost. Finally, in the *resolution*, the hero overcomes their burden against the odds.

All stories have this basic structure.

Another way to look at this is to note that all stories have a setting and characters. There is a main character who is also known as the hero or protagonist. It is usually this person we, as readers, want to see succeed throughout the plot. The story begins with an orientation, where we are introduced to the characters and their central conflict. The conflict is the source of a series of complications that occur within the plot and rising action towards the climax. The story ends at the resolution. Not all works of fiction actually feel like things have been 'resolved', despite the term for this part of a story.

All of our storylines basically unfold in these ways, however, there are particular features that allow us to sort narratives into seven types. The seven stories have their own specific conflict and pathway to resolution.

As we have established, there are seven basic plots in the stories we humans tell – and these are hardwired into our brains.

And here is our big reveal – the seven plots:

1. **Overcoming the monster**
2. **Rags to riches**
3. **The quest**
4. **Comedy**
5. **Tragedy**
6. **Rebirth**
7. **Journey and return**

The following chapters will outline each of the plots and exemplify them with a story. Other examples are offered, as well as ideas about how these might play out in real life.

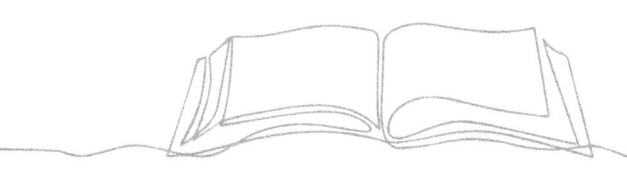

Overcoming the Monster

In this narrative, the protagonist must defeat a force that threatens their world, built up in the plot to appear monstrous and undefeatable. The task to overcome the monster is enormous. A fight must happen. There will be a winner and a loser in this story; think *Jaws* or *King Kong*.

THE PLOT

Anticipation stage: the threat has revealed itself in the protagonist's life/world. The protagonist may have been challenged to take on the monster by someone else or they may have determined the threat on their own and decided the monster needed to be overcome. The monster starts to be defined and its threat slowly revealed. The monster is ugly; it's strong and powerful. The potential for overcoming the monster seems implausible.

Dream stage: The monster is far off or distanced in some way and the protagonist seems to be well endowed to match the monster should confrontation arise. The threat does not seem great.

Frustration stage: it turns out the monster has far greater reach and ability to impact the protagonist than first thought. The protagonist is suffering the impact of the monster, and potentially those the protagonist cares about are affected as well. This threat causes daily struggles. The difficulty builds and the monster begins to appear undefeatable.

Nightmare stage: this is the stage of the story where all seems lost. The monster's strength and ability to adversely impact the protagonist and those they love is too great. The power base is too large and there is no way the protagonist can defeat this monster.

Miraculous escape: due to the strength, skills and ingenuity of the protagonist and because they are good and the monster is evil, the protagonist triumphs. The monster is defeated or has lost its ability to impact the protagonist and their people.

The Three Little Pigs is a fairy tale, like many fairy tales, where the protagonist must overcome the monster. Whilst all protagonists put hard work into preparing for their confrontations, in this story, the protagonist defeats the monster not through brute strength as Hercules does in his final quest but through ingenuity and hard work.

THE THREE LITTLE PIGS

Once upon a time there were three little pigs. They were being harassed by a big, bad wolf who threatened to make them his dinner on a daily basis. The threat was menacing but idle, until he grew tired of terrorising them from afar and began to close in on where they lived.

The pigs decided that building a house would provide them with the security they needed to keep themselves safe from the monster.

The first pig decided a house of straw would be just the thing. He could build it quickly and it would keep him safe.

The second pig favoured sticks. It would take a little longer, but he would be happier having something a little more solid between himself and the possibility of becoming something's tucker.

The third pig was prepared to knuckle down and build something a little more substantial. He determined that nothing less than bricks and mortar would make him feel safe against the wolf.

And so, the pigs went about their business of building their homes.

They were well ensconced in their humble homes when the wolf came a-calling. The first house he came upon was the one made of straw.

'Little pig, little pig, let me in,' chanted the wolf.

'Not by the hair of my chinny, chin, chin,' replied the pig. Suddenly he felt building something a little more substantial might have been the way to go. A wall of straw between him and the breath of this beast suddenly felt like nothing at all.

'Then I will huff, and I will puff, and I'll blow your house down!' shouted the wolf.

So he huffed. And he puffed. And with an almighty blow the little pig's house came apart, rendering him helpless against the attack of the wolf.

Although lamenting the loss of their sibling, the other pigs felt very happy that their houses were made of something more substantial than straw.

When the hunger came upon the wolf once more, he made his way to the house of sticks. He could smell the piggy flesh through the twigs and began to salivate.

'Little pig, little pig, let me in!' the wolf called menacingly.

'Not by the hair of my chinny, chin, chin,' replied the pig.

'Then I will huff, and I will puff, and I'll blow your house down!' shouted the wolf.

And so he huffed. And he puffed. And with an extra almighty blow this little pig's house came apart, leaving the little pig and his chin hair quivering. A perfect piggy treat for the wolf.

The last pig was nervous. Both of his siblings had become fodder for the wolf. However, he felt very satisfied to have put the extra graft into building the house from brick. The pig knew, though, the real test was yet to come.

By the by, the wolf became hungry and he came for another feed. He sniffed around the brick house and was frustrated at the lack of delicious porcine aroma.

Quick to anger, he shouted, 'Little pig, little pig, let me in!'

'Not by the hair of my chinny, chin, chin,' replied the pig.

'Then I will huff, and I will puff, and I'll blow your house down!' shouted the wolf.

And so he huffed. And he puffed. And with an extra, extra almighty blow he gave all he could to the little pig's house.

And nothing happened.

He tried again.

And so he huffed. And he puffed. And he huffed and he puffed. Huff, puff, huff, puff, huff, puff. And he BLEW. And with this extra, extra, extra, extra almighty blow he gave more than he thought he could to the little pig's house.

It remained standing.

The wolf was INCENSED. He couldn't believe this house was holding him back from his next piggy feed. He circled the house. He looked down. He looked sideways Then he looked up. And THEN he saw the chimney. He couldn't hide the grin on his face. Saliva escaped from his lips and his mouth held rows of sharp, fearsome teeth. The pig could see him through the window and a shudder shook him, tremors wobbling through his piggy fat.

The wolf scaled the house to get to the roof. The piggy got wind of what was happening and quickly lit a fire in the fireplace. The wolf climbed down and landed in the blazing fire. His fur caught fire and the horrible smell of burning dog hair filled the room. The wolf clambered and climbed and eventually got back up the chimney, down from the roof and ran off howling, his fur still ablaze.

The little pig was safe.

OVERCOMING THE MONSTER IN OUR LIVES

There are so many occasions where we can see ourselves pitted against the monster in real life. This applies when there is a one-off challenge at hand. The challenge is between yourself and the monster. We attribute an ugliness to the monster and the ugliness is likely to present on the inside. We build up the strength and power of this monster; we attribute to it almost superhuman powers and the potential for overcoming the monster seems implausible.

We can remain positive in applying this story to our lives if we maintain our focus on the 'prize'; the reward for being triumphant in the tale. We need to feel empowered with personal strength, courage and ingenuity, and be prepared to prepare for success to productively apply this story in a real life situation. If we have experiences in our lives where we have felt triumphant over a 'monster' we may have prior reference which allows us to feel empowered to succeed in any new, threatening situation.

When we are telling ourselves stories in the vein of overcoming the monster, we are constantly pitting ourselves against forces greater than us and this is overwhelming. It can 'grind us down' because of how disempowering it feels to be pitted against a force as strong as the monster. When we are under the greatest threat – the *nightmare stage* – we cannot see how we could possibly defeat the monster. This is a mentally unhealthy place to be in. We either need to find the tools to be able to overcome the threat or we will need to reframe the story for our own survival.

We must also be aware that overcoming the monster means that the narrative requires a winner and a loser.

Whilst, in many circumstances this is appropriate, it does not apply to all.

Real world applications of this story are vast but consider such life experiences as overcoming an addiction, dealing with a difficult boss, fighting illness, overcoming grief or depression, and surviving domestic violence situations.

Rags to riches

In the rags to riches narrative, the protagonist in this narrative is a modest, downtrodden character who is insignificant and overlooked. It may be that they have a hidden beauty, intelligence or skill set but they are seen as too young, too powerless or too poor to have any impact on the world.

The protagonist needs to knuckle down; to remain true to their values and work hard in this narrative.

Somewhere in the plot the protagonist has an experience that elevates them or reveals this hidden nature, proving them to be in some way exceptional. Think *Cinderella, Oliver Twist* or *The Ugly Duckling*.

THE PLOT

Initial wretchedness: the protagonist is initially young or in some way unlearned and naïve. They are in a miserable state and usually located in their home or natural environment. They are overshadowed by malevolent characters such as adults who oppress them and peers who target and bully them.

The call: the protagonist receives some kind of impetus to move out into the world, to flee the nest – to address their circumstances.

Initial success: the protagonist experiences some kind of success that foreshadows their later success and gives glimpses of their hidden talent, skills or beauty.

Central crisis: everything goes wrong. That which has been attained or glimpsed now seems further away than ever. Overwhelmed with despair, dark shadows return. A dark figure from the past might return, or the hero might lose their love interest either through physical separation or from a mental/ emotional standpoint. The small victories are stripped away, and the protagonist is at their lowest point in the story.

Independence and final ordeal: as they emerge from the crisis the hero can be seen in a new light; their new strength or beauty is becoming recognisable. They then face the dark figure – human or other – that stands between them and their goal. They resolve this, remove the dark shadow and can move into the final phase.

Final union, completion and fulfilment: the protagonist has everything come together for them. They are complete and whole; their success will project into the future and they will live happily ever after. The protagonist uses their own wits and skill to overcome their obstacle and reveal their previously hidden or only glimpsed ability or beauty.

Rags to riches is a common motif in our world. When we tell stories and we want the reader to vie for the protagonist, nothing works better than a real underdog story such as this. We are absolute suckers for an underdog. There are many biographical and autobiographical stories that reflect this story structure. JK Rowling's story fits very nicely.

JK ROWLING:
A REAL-LIFE RAGS TO RICHES STORY

Joanne Rowling (later to become JK by arbitrarily ascribing herself her grandmother's name) was a single mother living on welfare with a big idea. She had developed this idea some years before and had started writing, but only had a small amount of the work put down in the early phase of creation.

Tragedy struck Rowling as an adult when she lost her mother to a ten-year long battle with multiple sclerosis. This threw Rowling into grief and regret: despite writing the novel, she had never told her mother of it. It seems this intimate understanding of grief is channelled strongly through her protagonist – the orphan.

Rowling had earlier moved to Portugal where she taught the English language, married and had her child. The relationship was abusive and the marriage did not last long after the birth of Rowling's daughter.

Returning to England to be near her family, Rowling had three chapters of her book in her suitcase. She signed up for welfare and described herself as being '(as) poor as it is possible to be in modern Britain, without being homeless.'

Rowling would take her baby out for a walk in the pram, which encouraged her to sleep. She would then go to one of her favourite cafes where the coffee would keep flowing and the baby slept. She wrote her manuscript for her book longhand.

This book was entitled *Harry Potter and the Philosopher's Stone*.

Twelve publishing houses rejected the manuscript. But all the hard graft eventually paid off. This book was Rowling's golden ticket. The Harry Potter franchise is now estimated to be worth US$15 billion. JK is the highest paid living author in the country and in fact her personal fortune is amongst the highest in England. She would personally be much richer but she gives away a significant portion of her earnings to charity – a phenomenal philanthropist.

RAGS TO RICHES IN OUR LIVES

In the real world, this applies to anyone with an undeniably incredible talent who wants to break through and be successful. This could apply to photographers, musicians or artists but it could also simply apply in a work situation, where we are not being recognised through pay rises and promotions (or simply for doing a great job).

It is useful in narrating to ourselves stories that involve hard and apparently thankless work to overcome adversity or oppression. We can assure ourselves that we will eventually be rewarded and that our talents will be made apparent in due course.

This can help us to be patient and maintain our values as we plug away through tough times in anticipation of a big break. We do need to be mindful not to allow ourselves to leave things up to our fairy godmother; that we recognise the need to be proactive in making our opportunities happen. We also risk becoming very reactive when we do not get the 'happy ever after' result we were expecting for having knuckled down to hard work or having put up with oppressive circumstances.

As illustrated by the tale above, so many inspiring real-life stories apply this plot structure – people who have come from poverty or difficult circumstances and have become great successes.

The quest

In a quest, the protagonist and companions set out to acquire an important object or to get to a location. They face temptations and other obstacles along the way – it is a long haul. The companions usually supply some kind of complimentary skill set that supports the overcoming of the obstacles and temptations while supporting the achievement of the ultimate goal.

The protagonist needs to be prepared for a long haul, a big effort, with repeated challenges along the way. Each of these challenges helps the protagonist to develop the skills and capacity for the final overcoming.

Think *Harry Potter and the Philosopher's Stone* or *Watership Down*.

THE PLOT

The call: life has become oppressive and intolerable. The hero can correct this through embarking on an arduous and life threatening journey. In fiction, the protagonist may receive supernatural or visionary direction toward this life-renewing goal.

The journey: the hero embarks with one or more sidekicks. These can be: an unidentified group (this usually means they are likely to be sacrificed during ordeals along the way); a single faithful companion who supports all the protagonist endures and the decisions they make with steadfast piousness; or a companion who is placed in opposition to the hero, highlighting the protagonist's goodness and heroism by acting as their opposite. Or the hero can be accompanied by a group of companions who have complimentary skills to assist in overcoming ordeals. The characters themselves may demonstrate flaws that need to be overcome or learning that needs to take place for them to achieve their quest. They may also commit a series of errors linked to their character flaws. The journey then becomes ordeals whereby the character learns from these errors until they no longer make them. The ordeals include ghastly monsters, enticing temptations, or the possible need to travel between two opposite or oppressive forces (the rock and a hard place). There is a cycle of ordeal followed by respite. There is the presence of helpers, other than the travelling companions, who facilitate the hero's recovery, respite and capacity to achieve their goals or overcome the ordeals ahead.

Arrival and frustration: the ultimate goal is in sight, but a new series of obstacles have arisen.

The final ordeals: usually in sets of three, the hero must overcome this last set of obstacles before achieving the goal. These are often character tests to prove worthiness and the final battle is usually the most threatening.

The goal: after the thrilling escape in the final ordeal, the hero gets the life-transforming treasure. Life is beautiful and peaceful and the hero has secured their kingdom/love interest/accolades/a wonderful elixir...

An example of a myth told in the form of a quest is the story of *Hercules* or *Heracles*, depending on whether you are Greek or Roman respectively. Although the story varies in the telling, the following is an example of a quest with Hercules as our hero. We follow the hero as he pits himself – with all his strength and ingenuity – against seemingly mammoth tasks. He commits to the lengthy journey and enlists help when he needs it. He never takes his eye off the end game, which for him is to feel better about himself.

THE STORY OF HERCULES

Hercules is the son of Zeus to a mortal woman who was his lover. Zeus' wife, Hera, was crazy jealous and wanted to kill Hercules as he was the product of Zeus' union with another woman. She made it her personal mission to destroy this child. Hera sent two snakes into Hercules' crib, he played with them and then killed them. It seemed that this child, the product of human and god, was endowed with superhuman strength; he was, indeed, a demigod.

Hera's jealousy led her to interfere in many ways throughout Hercules' life. She never let go of her mission. When Hercules married and had children, Hera imbued him with insanity and he killed them. Hercules' life became untenable. He became overwhelmed with guilt and pleaded with the gods to punish him for his crime.

Hercules sought advice from the Oracle of Delphi who said he must serve King Eurystheus for ten years and complete any task he set for him as this would absolve him of both his crime and his guilt. The tasks were known as his twelve labours – this was the commencement of Hercules' quest.

Seeking help to prepare himself for the ordeals to come, Hercules trained under Philoctetes. Philoctetes then accompanied him on some of these challenges.

Hercules' first labour was to kill the Nemean Lion, a beast that had been striking terror in the people of the countryside nearby. The Lion had an impermeable hide and previous attempts to stop it had been fruitless. Hercules chased the Nemean Lion and trapped it in a cave. He strangled the beast with his bare hands then skinned it, wearing its skin as a suit of armour from then on.

Upon Hercules' return, the King prepared the second task. Hercules was to slay the Hydra. The Hydra was a beast with many hungry heads, each one blowing poison from its fangs, and when one hideous snake-like head was cut off, two more would grow back in its place. Hercules defeated the Hydra by enlisting the assistance of his nephew, who quickly seared with fire the cut made by severing the beast's heads, so the head would not grow back. Hercules then harvested and saved the poison from the beast's fangs, adding it to his arsenal.

Athena, the goddess of the hunt, had a large deer as a pet. The King coveted the deer. A desirable prize for its golden horns and hoofs of bronze, it was faster than any other creature alive. Hercules was charged with bringing the huge deer back to the King. He chased the animal for many months. Eventually, he shot an arrow that wounded it. Carrying the animal on his shoulders, he came upon Athena. She was shocked and dismayed to see her deer in its state of injury. When Hercules explained why he was forced to capture the animal, and demonstrated remorse, Athena forgave him. She allowed him to carry the animal back to the king after she healed its wounds, on the proviso that Hercules would afterwards set it free. Hercules fulfilled his task.

The following assignment involved the capture of a fearsome boar with a bad temper and long, piercing tusks. Daily, the boar would come lumbering down the ridge, attacking and killing everything in its path. Hercules chased the boar into a deep pile of snow, trapped it in a net and carried the net with the beast inside back to King Eurystheus, the fourth labour completed.

For the fifth labour, Eurystheus ordered Hercules to clean up King Augeas' stables. Augeas was very rich, and he had many herds of cows, bulls, goats, sheep and horses. This was a mammoth task – there were thousands of beasts. Seeing how effective Hercules had been in completing earlier tasks, he added another layer of difficulty: Eurystheus expected Hercules to clean up after the beasts of Augeas in a single day. Augeas' son accompanied him on this task to bear witness to the feat.

Hercules came up with a plan to effect this cleansing. He would use the natural environment to assist. First the hero tore a big opening in the wall of the cattle-yard where the stables were. Then he made another opening in the wall on the opposite side of the yard. Afterward, he dug wide trenches to two rivers which flowed nearby. He turned the course of the rivers into the yard. The rivers rushed through the stables, flushing them out, and all the mess flowed out of the hole in the wall on the other side of the yard. The task was complete.

The next labour was to kill the Stymphalian birds. These were murderous birds with claws and beaks as sharp as metal and feathers that flew like darts. Hercules scared them out of their nests with a rattle and then killed them with poison arrows he had made from the Hydra's poison.

The seventh labour was to capture the Cretan Bull. Hercules sailed to Crete, where the bull had been wreaking havoc by uprooting crops and levelling orchard walls. Hercules stole up behind the bull. He used his hands to choke it (stopping before it was killed), and then shipped it back to the King. Eurystheus, fearful, hid in his *pithos* at the first sight of the creature. He released the bull and it continued its reign of terror in its new location.

For his eighth challenge, Hercules had to steal the Mares of Diomedes. He was unaware that the horses were wild and maddened because of their predilection for human flesh and their inability to feed their desire. They were all kept harnessed to a bronze manger. Hercules managed to free the horses and cornered them on a peninsula. He then trapped them, by digging a trench and filling it with water, turning the peninsula into an island. When Diomedes arrived, Hercules killed him and fed him to the horses. This becalmed the horses and Hercules managed to bring them to Eurystheus who left the newly calmed horses to roam the countryside.

The next challenge for Hercules was to steal the girdle of the Amazon queen, Hippolyta. He had charmed her and convinced her to hand over the girdle but Hera interfered and turned the queen against Hercules. He was forced to slay her and tore the girdle from her body, presenting it to the King.

As a tenth labour, Eurystheus commanded that Hercules fetch the red cattle of Geryon. Geryon was a terrifying monster with three heads and three sets of legs that lived on the island of Erythia. Hercules killed Geryon, as well as the monster's two headed watchdog, Orthos, before successfully escaping with the herd of red cattle.

Labour number eleven had Hercules bring to Eurystheus the golden apples which belonged to Zeus, King of the gods. Hera had given these apples to Zeus as a wedding gift and the apples were kept in a garden at the northern edge of the world. They were guarded by a hundred-headed dragon and by the Hesperides, nymphs who were daughters of Atlas (the titan who held the sky and the earth upon his shoulders). Hercules happened upon Atlas and offered to hold the earth for him to give him a spell if Atlas would, in return, get the golden fruit for him. Atlas agreed, collecting the fruit and returning them to Hercules, who had to trick the recently freed titan back into holding up the earth.

The final labour was the most intense and dangerous. Eurystheus ordered Hercules to go to the Underworld – the world of the dead – and kidnap Cerberus, its guard dog. Cerberus was a vicious beast and a strange mixture of creatures: he had three heads of wild dogs, a dragon tail, and heads of snakes all over his back. Before making the trip to the Underworld, Hercules decided that he should take some extra precautions, knowing that once in the kingdom of Hades he might not be allowed to leave and re-join the living. The hero visited Eumolpus who initiated Hercules into the Eleusinian Mysteries which was supposed to protect him in the underworld (after he met the conditions of membership). Hercules made his way down to the Underworld encountering monsters, heroes, and ghosts as he journeyed through. Finally, he found Pluto and asked the god for Cerberus. The master of the Underworld allowed Hercules to take Cerberus with him, only if he overpowered the beast with nothing more than his own strength.

A weaponless Hercules set off to find Cerberus. Near the gates of Acheron, one of the five rivers of the Underworld, Hercules encountered Cerberus. The hero wrapped his arms around the beast, grabbing all three necks at once, and wrestled Cerberus into submission. Cerberus fought but had to submit to the force of the hero, and Hercules brought Cerberus to Eurystheus.

The King was so afraid of the beast that he released Hercules from his labours with the proviso he returned Cerberus to his home in the underworld.

Freed at last, Hercules' life remained tormented by Hera and he was never free of his guilt. Eventually, after suffering for so long, Hercules threw himself on a funeral pyre. The mortal part of him burned away, leaving only that which was immortal and allowing him to take his place in Olympus with the gods.

THE QUEST IN OUR LIVES

The quest as a lived experience involves being in the journey for the long haul. As illustrated by Hercules' story, this is a saga. It goes on and on. The protagonist of the quest is someone who accepts help along the way and seeks learning as well as drawing on the strengths of others to help achieve their ultimate goal. The hero of the quest may be distracted from their final goal at times – sometimes for long periods – but the goal remains in place and they battle along off and on until they are ultimately triumphant.

Quests can occur in our lives in many ways, for example the completion of an educational qualification, a weight loss journey, or overcoming a health condition. If we cannot find the stamina for the long haul, be able to build on the successes we find along the way, or be willing to seek and accept help, we will find the quest a very difficult narrative indeed. We need to keep our self-talk positive, be persistent, seek help and expect a lengthy journey for this narrative to work for us.

Comedy

The comedy is a narrative that focuses on confusion and hidden truths; it nestles in blindness to the truths around us. Comedy does not necessarily have to be laugh out loud funny, but it does not often take itself seriously. Having said that, the confusion and irony can be exceptionally frustrating and upsetting. However, we can be sure of a 'happy' ending in comedy, an ending where everything turns out for the best. An adverse circumstance may exist and the conflict can become very convoluted as the confusion ties everything in knots, but everything ends well with all loose ends tied up. This is the happy ending narrative.

The pathway to the happy ending is in revealing the truth of the situation.

Think most romance films, eg *Muriel's Wedding, Four Weddings and a Funeral* or *Bridget Jones's Diary*.

THE PLOT

Confusion: The story commences with characters in a world shadowed by confusion, uncertainty, frustration and miscommunication. There is something unknown or misunderstood and the characters are shut off from each other. Nothing is clear. A central, dark figure may be the cause of the confusion and this character either acts unseeingly or without heart. Quite often there is self-delusion or a lack of self-awareness on the behalf of the protagonist. Other times it is a general state of confusion.

Confusion compounds: things become disastrous and a happy ending seems impossible. Everything is so confused that it seems tied up in knots. It seems irredeemable.

Denouement: this is directly translated as 'untying' and is the part of the plot where the truths are revealed. The protagonist comes to a new understanding of self and others, confusion is allayed, true identities are revealed, the love interests find each other, and the dark figure reveals and redeems themselves. Everything turns out for the best and there is a 'happily ever after'.

Jane Austen's *Pride and Prejudice* is a classic telling of a story through the comedy plot. So much mistaken and prejudicial judgement of character leads to confusion and distance between the love interests. All is resolved beautifully in the end with the relevant couples marrying and living happily ever after.

PRIDE AND PREJUDICE

Mr. Bennet of Longbourn estate has five daughters but his property is entailed and can only be passed to a male heir. His wife also lacks an inheritance, so his family will be destitute upon his death. Thus, it is imperative that at least one of the girls marry well to support the others, which is the motivation that drives the plot. The novel revolves around the importance of marrying for love rather than money or social prestige, despite the communal pressure to make a wealthy match. Mrs Bennet is very keen to see her five daughters Jane, Elizabeth, Mary, Kitty, and Lydia, married, and at least one 'married well'.

A wealthy young gentleman named Charles Bingley has rented the manor of Netherfield Park, which causes great interest in Longbourn, particularly in the Bennet household. In the interests of this, Mr. Bennet pays a social visit to Mr. Bingley. Following this, the Bennet family attend a ball at which Mr. Bingley is present. He is drawn to Jane, spending the evening attending to and dancing with her. Mr Darcy, his aloof and apparently disdainful friend, however, shows displeasure with the evening and a displeasing countenance. This is furthered by his refusal to dance with Elizabeth, impacting his reputation amongst the attendees. He becomes a subject of the post-event gossip.

At social functions over subsequent weeks, however, Mr. Darcy finds himself increasingly attracted to Elizabeth's charm and intelligence. Jane's friendship with Mr. Bingley also continues to prosper, and Jane pays a visit to the Bingley mansion. On her journey to the house she is caught in a downpour and catches ill, forcing her to stay at Netherfield, among the Bingleys, for several days. In order to tend to Jane, Elizabeth rambles through muddy fields and arrives with a splattered dress, much to the contempt of the snobbish Miss Bingley (Charles Bingley's sister). Miss Bingley's spite only increases when she notices that Darcy, whom she is chasing, pays quite a bit of heed to Elizabeth.

A young local clergyman, Mr Collins, stands to inherit the Bennet's family home. Having a vested interest, this pompous young man sniffs around the Bennet sisters, hoping to catch himself a lovely wife. He is immediately interested in Elizabeth and proposes in haste. However, Elizabeth is not at all interested in Mr Collins, in fact she found him distasteful. Elizabeth wants to marry for love and immediately turns him down, which insults him greatly.

A local military squad is stationed nearby and this captures the interest of the Bennet girls. A soldier, by the name of Wickham, is friendly toward Elizabeth and spins tales about Mr Darcy, suggesting that Darcy was responsible for cheating him out of an inheritance. This further turns Elizabeth against Darcy, creating more distance between them and making their relationship even less likely.

Winter comes and the Bingley siblings and Mr Darcy close up the house and return to London, disappointing Jane who was sincere in her liking for Mr Bingley and was hoping that a proposal would materialise from the relationship. More news arrives, Mr Collins is engaged to Charlotte Lucas, threatening the Bennet family's inheritance. Charlotte is in need of a husband and explains her situation to Elizabeth, who kindly maintains her friendship with Charlotte, despite what appears to be a conflict.

Jane makes a trip to London during the winter, hoping to progress her relationship with Mr Bingley. However, a disappointing visit with his sister resulted in Miss Bingley telling Jane she was not fit for Mr Bingley and poor Jane left without seeing him at all.

It appears as if none of the Bennet girls will be wed!

Elizabeth visits her friend, Charlotte, regularly in her marital home. It turns out that Mr Collins' benefactor, Lady Catherine, is a nearby neighbour and the Aunt of Mr Darcy. A chance encounter makes Mr Darcy aware of Elizabeth's regular presence at the Collins' and Mr Darcy finds reasons to also be present at the home.

Mr Darcy makes a proposal of marriage to Elizabeth, which comes as a surprise to the young woman. She refuses him on the basis of the personality he had shown Elizabeth and his tarnished character as a result of Wickham's tales. She specifically brings up the directing of Mr Bingley away from her sister, Jane, and the issue of Wickham's inheritance.

Leaving her at the time, Mr Darcy felt an urge to clear his reputation with Elizabeth and sends her a letter explaining himself. He explains that he urged Bingley to distance himself from Jane because he was looking out for her, thinking that Mr Bingley was not serious in his interest of the girl. He also called out Wickham as a liar, citing the true reason for their falling out was the planned elopement of Wickham with Mr Darcy's younger sister.

Elizabeth now sees Mr Darcy in a new light. She returns home from the Collins' and treats Wickham with deserved disdain.

The military men were leaving town, putting the Bennet girls into a tizz. Lydia manages to extract permission from her father to follow the regiment to Brighton and she was to stay with the old colonel. Elizabeth also travels, staying close by Mr Darcy's estate but she carefully avoids him.

On an occasion when she is sure Mr Darcy is absent, she visits his estate. She finds herself delighted with the property and his servants talk about what a generous and pleasant master he is, further shaping Elizabeth's positive feelings about Mr Darcy.

Unexpectedly, Mr Darcy arrives and treats Elizabeth genially. He invites Elizabeth to meet his sister.

Now comes a letter from home stating very bad news – Lydia has eloped with Wickham. No-one can find the pair and the fear is that they are living together out of wedlock; besmirching the family's reputation and ruining all the girls' chances of any marriage, let alone a good one.

Mr Bennet and Mr Gardiner go off in search of the couple. Their search proves fruitless and Mr Bennet returns home empty handed. The family are wretched until a letter arrives from Mr Gardiner saying he has found the couple and Wickham has agreed to the marriage in return for an annual stipend. The Bennets believe that this payment has been made by Mr Gardiner but

Elizabeth finds out that Mr Darcy is responsible for her family's salvation.

The arrival of the newlyweds to Longbourn is not well received by Mr Bennet and the couple soon embark on a journey to the north of England to Wickham's new assignment. Mr Bingley returns to the rented estate nearby and resumes courting Jane. Darcy also returns to stay with his friend. He visits with the Bennets but makes no reference to the previously made proposal.

Lady Catherine, however, corners Elizabeth and mentions that she has heard of her nephew's intention of marrying her. Lady Catherine states that she does not consider Elizabeth a suitable match for her nephew and tries to get Elizabeth to refuse his proposal when it comes. Elizabeth denies any evidence of any proposal being in current existence but also steadfastly refuses to put anything but her own happiness at the forefront of future decisions.

A later walking excursion involving Elizabeth and Mr Darcy results in them discussing his feelings. He explains that he still feels the same about her in this moment as he did when he made his initial proposal. Elizabeth accepts his proposal in a far gentler and fonder spirit than she had when she refused his previous proposal, having come to understand the true nature of her intended.

Elizabeth and Darcy marry and return to Darcy's estate, while Jane marries Bingley and remains close to Longbourn in the summer residence.

THE COMEDY IN OUR LIVES

When we tell ourselves stories in a comedic vein, there *can* be a light-heartedness about the narration, an ability not to take things too seriously. But there can also be a sense of absurdity about the circumstances that is not funny at all. It can be a positive, healthy and safe place from which to narrate our lives, so long as we don't fall into the trap of being passive and shaking our heads at our own folly or that of others. Of not being active or taking things seriously enough.

The absurd nature of the obscured truths and confusion which lead to frustration can be a significant issue, as we put our faith in the resolution that we expect is coming- once people finally see the reality of a situation and the truth of each person's character.

We must also take heed that happily ever after is a falsehood. This can lead us down the garden path of 'I will be happy when...' thinking. Grave disappointment can occur if we think that uncovering truths and resolving confusion means everything will turn out well in the end without any further work on our own behalf. One example of a happily ever after scenario is marriage. Anyone who has ever been married or in a relationship knows that tying the knot is just the beginning of the hard work of being together.

Love stories are only one example of how this plot might fit the narration of events in our real lives. Applying for a job, where we need to reveal the truth of ourselves to emerge victorious in the process is another example. So is trouble among colleagues and peers, where gossip has played a part or a work project where people are actually on the same page but their communication styles are making them feel like they are at odds with each other. In all these situations the comedy plot line matches real life. If we give things time for truths to be revealed (and failing that, help things along so truths can be exposed) the comedy plot can serve us. In the meantime, we feel the self-assurance that we are in the right, that it is just because we are misunderstood and the fact we have not got the full truth of ourselves out there which is hindering us. When we hold faith in our morals, this can be reassuring in our lives.

Tragedy

The tragedy is the story without the happy ending. The protagonist is a hero with a major character flaw or who makes a great mistake which is ultimately their undoing. Their unfortunate end evokes pity at their folly and the downfall of a fundamentally good character. Alternatively, the situation is fundamentally flawed.

The pathway forward in a tragedy is to accept that there is no improving or changing the situation, person or problem. We need to learn this, grieve, and move on.

Think *Bonnie and Clyde*, *The Picture of Dorian Gray* or *Romeo and Juliet*.

THE PLOT

Temptation: it begins with an initial mood of anticipation – something is going to happen for the protagonist. They establish their desire for something that seems to be 'missing', and therefore they have their focus.

Dream stage: the protagonist commences on their journey toward their goal. Everything seems to be going well. No one calls the protagonist out on their behaviour, thoughts, and motivations or if they do the protagonist does not heed the warnings.

Frustration stage: things start to go mysteriously wrong for the protagonist. These things might start off as minor annoyances, but they build. The decisions and actions taken by the protagonist cause a downward spiral toward their dark ending. A shadow figure significant to the plot may appear at this point (or in the case of Dorian Gray, earlier).

Nightmare stage: everything goes horrendously wrong. Despair grows, behaviour devolves and the hole gets deeper!

Death and destruction: the protagonist is destroyed either by their own hand or the forces they have unleashed. They die, kill themselves or are simply ruined.

Oscar Wilde's *The Picture of Dorian Gray* exemplifies the tragedy for us. The character starts off okay, although his only claim is irresistible beauty. Pretty soon he gives into temptation and goes down a dark path. It does not end well for Dorian Gray.

THE PICTURE OF DORIAN GRAY

Dorian Gray is a young and incredibly beautiful man who is enmeshed in London's society. He meets an artist, Basil Hallward, in the stately London home of Basil's aunt. Dorian Gray immediately captures the artist's eye and he has Dorian sit for several portraits. Hallward shows his work of Dorian to his good friend, Lord Henry Wootton. Wootton insists this is Hallward's best work and it needs to be displayed, however, Hallward is reluctant because he has strong feelings for Dorian Gray and fears the work is too revealing of his feelings for the subject. Wootton is a scandalous character and unashamedly celebrates youth, beauty and pleasure. He disagrees with Hallward and claims it is his masterpiece.

Dorian then arrives at the studio and Lord Wootton shares his beliefs with Dorian. Dorian is fascinated as Henry explains his belief that one should live life to the fullest by indulging one's impulses. Basil fears Lord Henry will have a damaging influence on the impressionable, young Dorian and it seems these fears are well founded. When Henry points out that beauty and youth are fleeting, Dorian curses his portrait which he believes will one day remind him of the beauty he lost. He declares that he would give his soul if the portrait were to grow old and wrinkled while he remained young and handsome.

Lord Henry expresses his desire to own the portrait but Basil insists the portrait belongs to Dorian. Dorian assumes ownership.

Lord Henry determines that he will influence the shape of Dorian's character. Dorian readily becomes a disciple of the 'new Hedonism' and resolves to live a life dedicated to the pursuit of pleasure.

Dorian falls in love with a young actress, Sibyl Vane. He adores her acting and she, in turn, refers to him as her 'Prince Charming'. Sybil's brother tried to warn her of the negative influence of Dorian but she was blinded by love. In fact, she was so profoundly affected by her love for

Dorian that her love for theatre began to pale in comparison. Sibyl decides that she can no longer act and gives up the stage.

Dorian's love for Sybil, however, is inextricably linked to her acting and her great ability. She no longer has the same appeal to him without her presence on the stage. In an act of cruelty, he breaks his engagement with her.

When Dorian returns home, he notices the face in his portrait has changed. It has a cruel and sneering expression. Shocked and frightened that his image in the painting bears the ill effects of his behaviour and evidence of his sins will be documented on the canvas, he determines to make amends with Sibyl. The following afternoon Lord Henry brings the terrible news that Sibyl has killed herself. In typical Lord Henry fashion, he encourages Dorian to see the death as far from his fault, rather to reframe the event as a sort of artistic triumph and put the matter behind him. Dorian also chooses to hide his portrait in a remote, upper room of his house to avoid witness of its transformation. Out of sight, out of mind.

Lord Henry then gives Dorian a book full of wicked exploits. For the next eighteen years it becomes Dorian's bible. He descends deeper into a life of vice. He devotes himself to harvesting new experiences and sensations with no regard for morals or consequences.

Dorian cultivates a negative reputation amongst polite society but his social circle continues to accept him because he remains young and beautiful. In the meantime, his image in the painting grows ever more hideous.

One night, Basil Hallward arrives at Dorian's home to confront him about the rumours that plague his reputation. They argue, and Dorian offers Basil a look at his soul, evidenced by the painting. When he shows Basil the now repugnant portrait, Basil is absolutely horrified. Fearing for Dorian's soul he begs Dorian to repent his sins. Dorian claims it is too late for penance and kills Basil in a fit of rage. His sins exacerbate, as in order to dispose of Basil's corpse Dorian blackmails an estranged friend (a doctor) whom he contrives to assist him with getting rid of Basil's body.

The night after the murder Dorian is in an opium den where he meets up with James Vane, Sybil's brother. James attempts to avenge the death of his sister but Dorian manages to escape to his country estate. Dorian is wracked by sudden guilt. While he is entertaining a hunting party, James arrives at the country estate. James is accidentally shot by the hunters and Dorian feels safe once more.

He resolves to amend his life and tells Lord Henry as much, stating that he will not take advantage of a young lady who is taken with him. Expecting this to have positively impacted his soul, Dorian returns to the portrait. Instead of reflecting an improvement in his character, the portrait has taken on a look of slyness. Furious, Dorian picks up the knife he used to stab Basil Hallward and stabs at the painting. His servants rush upstairs at the sound of crashing and screaming to find the portrait unharmed, showing as it was originally the portrait of a beautiful young man. On the floor lies an old man, loathsome in appearance; horribly wrinkled and disfigured, with a knife plunged into his heart. **(Spark notes 2021)**

THE TRAGEDY IN OUR LIVES

It is interesting to think that this plot line could be in any way useful to us narrating our stories. This narrative is about things not working out. It is about things never being able to be resolved. It is about loss, grieving, letting go and moving on. When the tragedy is the most appropriate telling of our stories, this is what we must do.

A challenge we all face when tragedy befalls us is that many of us have difficulty when we get held in the grief process of the tragedy. If, after a reasonable amount of time for grieving we cannot move past the extreme feelings associated with loss, we may need to shift our thinking to a new storyline because holding on to the narrative is impacting our ability to accommodate the loss into our lives and move into a new phase. Sometimes we need help with this, and our reframing may need to take the form of a quest – a commitment to overcoming the challenges associated with dealing with the grief situation.

We may also find that if we are quick to narrate experiences as a tragedy, we become quick to quit things when they become challenging – deciding it can't be done – and this may be before it is actually true.

In some circumstances, we are far better off simply shaking our heads at the folly of our fatally flawed friends while allowing them the space to live their own lives and make their own mistakes. In our own situation, it offers us a chance to let go of things and situations that are not redeemable, gives legitimacy to giving up where that is the choice that best serves us.

Real life situations, where the framing of the story as a tragedy may serve us, always take the form of a regrettable circumstance that we must give up as irredeemable. A failed marriage, bad family relationships, untenable work situations, toxic friendships, these can all be framed as tragedies allowing us to put them behind us and move on in our lives.

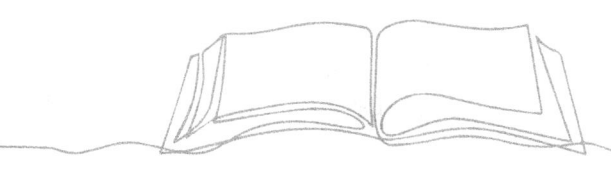

Rebirth

The rebirth involves the protagonist who is flawed. They need to look to themselves to find areas for change and improvement.

There is an event or set of circumstances that forces the main character to change their ways and often become a better individual. Think *Beauty and the Beast*, *A Christmas Carol* or *The Lorax*.

PLOT

The dark power: a young hero or heroine falls under a spell or is influenced by a dark power.

Dream stage: for a time, everything seems fine and the threat seems to have receded.

The threat returns: eventually the threat reapproaches in full force. The hero is imprisoned or trapped in a state of massive discomfort; held in the grip of the dark power.

Nightmare stage: this goes on for a long time and it seems the dark power has triumphed

Redemption: a miraculous redemption is effected usually through the influence of another character: a love interest, a child, the greater good or a wise person. The protagonist 'switches sides' or experiences a transformation that ensures a new and better state of being and living.

The movie *50 First Dates* (2004) is a contemporary example of a rebirth narrative. The hero, Henry Roth, falls under the spell of the gorgeous Lucy. He changes his ways to win her heart.

50 FIRST DATES

Henry Roth is a man afraid of commitment until he meets the beautiful Lucy. They hit it off and Henry thinks he has finally found 'the one'. Henry lives in Hawaii, working as a marine biologist at a Hawaiian sea world. He is a master 'player', seeing holiday makers in short-term relationships and making a big impression on all kinds of ladies and even a fella. He is commitment-phobic and shows some expertise in extricating himself from one-night stands. That is, until he meets Lucy Whitmore. His boat breaks and he travels to the shore by runabout finding a settlement. He goes into the local café and orders a feed while he waits for the coast guard to tow the boat. He spots Lucy in the café and feels the pull of interest, so he returns the next day and introduces himself. They spend hours together.

Both Henry and Lucy enjoy each other's company and feel the start of something. Before she goes, she invites him to breakfast the next day. Henry freaks out that night, realising he is interested in a local which could mean a relationship with the potential for a future so he tries a date with another holiday maker. He doesn't enjoy it and begs off.

Unfortunately, Lucy was in an accident that caused short-term memory loss. Every night while she sleeps the slate of her memory is wiped clean. When she wakes up in the morning she remembers everything that happened up to the moment of the accident but nothing that happened afterward.

Henry waits for Lucy in the café in the morning and becomes confused when she fails to recognise him. This is the point where Henry finds out from the café lady that Lucy suffers from memory loss and can't remember each day. The tattooed guy at the café tries to protect Lucy from Henry, but he agrees on a bet with Henry that he could get Lucy to eat with him again.

Henry tries every day to get Lucy to talk to him again. He comes across as pretty fake and she rejects him until he pretends he can't read and she takes pity on him. She sees through him eventually and flips him off. He becomes more creative about the ways in which he tries to get her to be interested in him each new day.

Conflict arises when her family questions Henry's interest in Lucy. Her dad and brother try to send him packing.

Over time, Henry starts to develop a more genuine interest in Lucy and looks for new and crazy ways to connect with her. These attempts are now based on genuine affection and knowledge of who she is as he gets to know her. Falling for Lucy is his catalyst for change and instead of seeking a new woman each night, he becomes determined to make Lucy fall in love with him every single day.

Lucy occasionally has a 'bad day', where she is exposed to the fact that she has memory loss. Her dad then has to take her through what has happened to her and she grieves for what transpired and what she has lost. Henry experiences her first bad day since meeting her and offers to take her to the doctor so she can talk to him. The whole family goes and Lucy's dad informs her she is 'sort of' dating Henry. At the close of the day, her dad decides Henry is okay and invites him for a beer.

Henry decides to try and help Lucy come to terms with each new day; the fact that time has passed since her accident with a whole lot of history she cannot retain. He makes a video to explain her world that she is to watch in the mornings, clarifying her situation and recent history, and then he gets her to fall in love with him again. The romance ramps up. He tells her he loves her. They have a lot of 'first' kisses! He writes her a song about their love story. Henry finally spends the night with Lucy and when they wake up she knocks him out. She overhears a conversation between her father and Henry, finding out about his plans to go to Alaska. She feels guilty about him abandoning his plans. She decides that having Henry stick around for her is unfair on him, there is too much that he has to put up with, even for love. She breaks up with him.

The commitment-phobe is rebirthed as someone driven to push this love affair forward and overcome the difficulties associated with Lucy's disability. His newly formed character involves him making choices that show a significant commitment to his love interest. Without Lucy in his life, he is celibate and wishing they were together. He decides it is too much to be in the same locale as Lucy and decides to leave the island.

Eventually Lucy moves to the institute – a residential facility for people with brain injury – to stop being a burden on her family. Henry decides to visit her and not rush to leave the island. She doesn't remember him, but she shows him her art studio which is full of portraits of him. She said she dreams of him every night.

She agrees to marry him and the devoted husband and (father!) finds ways of catching her up on what has happened in her life up to that point every morning when she wakes up.

BEN FINDS SOMETHING INSIDE HIMSELF

This story comes from *Success through a Positive Mental Attitude*, a book by Napoleon Hill and W. Clement Stone. It is such an apt illustration of a rebirth story that I felt compelled to include it. I cannot tell you if the story is a true one, although it reads as such. The main character, Ben, suffers the brutality of bullies. However, he finds a way of changing himself. He finds inspiration from some stories he has read and reimagines himself as someone strong and brave. He changed himself, particularly his thinking, and he changed his life.

Ben grew up in a near-slum neighbourhood in St Joseph, Missouri. His father was an immigrant tailor who earned little money. Many days there simply wasn't enough to eat. To heat the small home, Ben used to take a coal scuttle, and walk down the railroad tracks that ran nearby. There he would pick up pieces of coal. It embarrassed Ben to have to do it. He'd often try to sneak through the back streets so children from school wouldn't see him.

But they often did. There was one gang of boys in particular who found great sport in ambushing Ben on his way home from the tracks and beating him up. They would scatter his coal all over the street and send him home with tears streaming from his eyes. Thus it was that Ben lived in more or less a permanent state of fear and self-despising.

Something happened, as it always must when we break the pattern of defeat. The victory within us does not assert itself until we are ready. Ben was inspired to positive action because he read a book. It was Robert Cloverdale's Struggle by Horatio Alger.

In it, Ben read the adventures of a youngster like himself who was faced with great odds, but who overcame these odds with the courage and moral strength which Ben wished to possess.

The boy read every one of the Horatio Alger books he could borrow. As he read, he lived the part of the hero. All winter he sat in the cold kitchen reading stories of courage and success, unconsciously absorbing a Positive Mental Attitude.

Some months after he read his first Horatio Alger book, Ben Cooper was again making a trip down the railroad tracks. Off in the distance, he saw three figures dart behind a building. His first thought was to turn and run. Then he remembered the courage that he had admired in his book heroes, and, instead of turning, his hand gripped the coal scuttle more tightly and he marched straight ahead, as if he were one of Horatio Alger's heroes.

It was a brutal fight. The three boys jumped Ben all at the same time. His bucket dropped, and he started flailing his arms with a determination that caught the bullies by surprise. Ben's right hand smashed into the lips and nose of one of the boys – his left hand into his stomach. To Ben's surprise, the boy stopped fighting and turned and ran. The other two boys were hitting and kicking him. Ben managed to push one boy away with his knees and knock the other down. He jumped on the second boy with his knees while he plowed punch af-

ter punch into his stomach and jaw – as if he were mad. Now there was just one boy left. This was the leader. He had jumped on top of Ben. Ben managed to pull him aside and get on his feet. For a second the two boys stood and looked at each other squarely in the eyes.

And then, bit by bit, the leader stepped backwards. He, too, ran away. Perhaps it was righteous indignation, but Ben picked up a chunk of coal and threw it at the retreater.

It wasn't until then that Ben realised that his nose was bleeding and that he had black and blue marks on his body from the punches and kicks he received. It was worth it! It was a great day in Ben's life. In that moment he had overcome fear.

Ben Cooper wasn't much stronger than he had been a year earlier. His attackers were no less tough. The difference came in Ben's positive mental attitude. He had faced danger in spite of fear. He decided that no longer was he going to be pushed around by bullies. **(Success through a Positive Mental Attitude, Napoleon Hill & W. Clement Stone, pp.20-22)**

*Reproduced with permission from the Napoleon Hill Foundation.

THE REBIRTH NARRATIVE IN REAL LIFE

The rebirth story plays out in real life when we realise we need to change something about ourselves in order to live a better life. Sometimes we need a push to realise 'something has to change, there is a better way'. But once we are awakened to our need to change and we begin the process of transforming ourselves, everything else becomes that much easier because we're more open to long-lasting change.

Be wary of falling into the habit of thinking changing ourselves is the only answer. This can lead to 'flightiness' or a lack of 'stickability'. We need to make sure that we commit to changes long enough to see if they are the right thing to do before we embark on the newest, greatest change. And sometimes we should start on small changes and look for the impact as a guide of what to do next. We can also begin to perceive ourselves as being 'not enough', of having lesser value or falling short in some way. Make sure that the right pathway in this particular life situation truly involves a personal change and that we are not falling victim of a neurosis, where we are taking responsibility where responsibility is not due.

However, if it is clear that we need to effect some change, if we are very positive about this possibility for change and we are willing to work on ourselves, the rebirth narrative can serve us very well. Consider times when our lack of study is resulting in poor grades, times when we are not spending enough quality time with our children and they are going off the rails, when our mother is not talking to us because we haven't made the effort to see her lately or when our boss is dragging us into the office for having too many sick days. Recognising the need for change and then implementing these changes results in a better life for us.

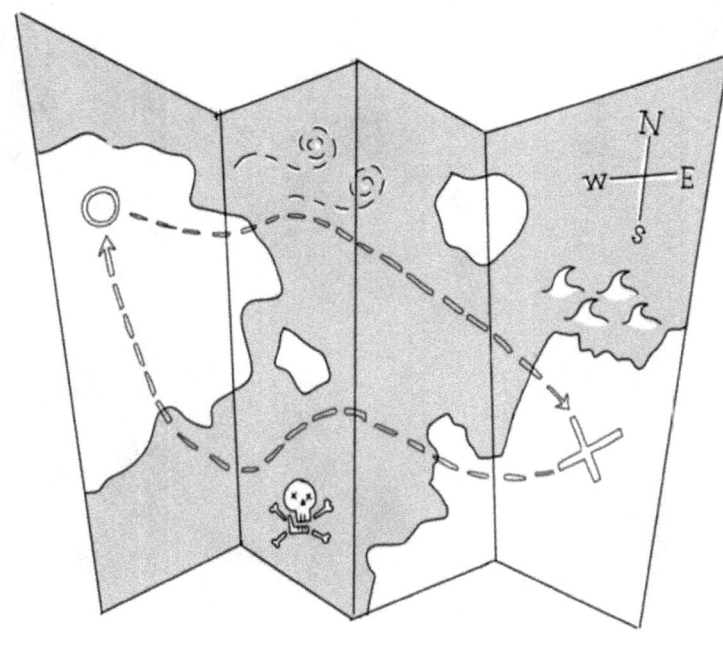

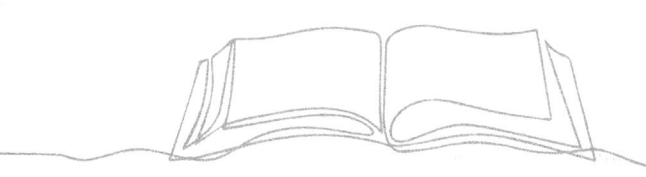

Journey and Return

In the journey and return, the protagonist goes to a strange land or is in a world very different to their own which is overwhelming and strange. Then, after overcoming the threats it poses or learning important lessons unique to that location, they return with experience which helps them to live better in their own world. Think *Alice in Wonderland*, *Back to the Future* or *Ragnarok*.

THE PLOT

Anticipation stage and the fall into the other world: the protagonist is in some way restricted and for some reason open to a life-changing experience. They may be young and naïve, actively curious, bored or reckless. They are suddenly moved out of their familiar, comfortable world into one that is strange, alien, and unlike their previous experiences.

Dream stage: the initial exploration of the new place is disconcerting but can be positive because of its unique differences. However, it remains uncomfortable and unfamiliar, and the protagonist will still feel the pull toward home.

Frustration stage: the adventure becomes difficult and frustrations arise. A darkness intrudes and becomes increasingly concerning.

Nightmare stage: the darkness becomes seriously threatening to the protagonist's survival.

Thrilling escape and return: when it becomes unbearable or the protagonist looks sure to fail, they successfully and miraculously escape. They return home renewed, having grown as a person as a result of the journey. The change in the character does not guarantee a happy ending, just a changed character who can then apply that change to living better in their home world.

In the story of *Alice in Wonderland* she is transported into a strange and confusing world where she is constantly trying to make sense of things. The journey for Alice is one of a child trying to make sense of the adult world. Her realisation is that for her to be able to cope in an adult world she needs to understand and come to terms with the rules of that world.

ALICE IN WONDERLAND

Alice, a young girl, is off picnicking with her sister. Bored, she falls asleep and dreams of a white rabbit who pulls a watch from his waistcoat and says, 'I am late.'

Alice follows the White Rabbit and finds herself down a rabbit hole – she finds herself in a strange, new world.

Immediately Alice comes upon a vast hallway lined with doors. She finds a small door that she opens using a key she discovers on a nearby table. She could see a beautiful garden through the keyhole but cries when she realises she cannot fit through the door. A bottle appears marked 'drink me', and so she does. Alice then shrinks down to the right size to enter the door but now cannot enter because she has left the key on the table which is way above her. Alice finds a cake with a sign saying 'eat me'. Alice consumes the cake and she grows exceptionally large. She still cannot get into the garden and starts crying once more.

Alice's giant tears pool at her feet. Still crying, Alice shrinks and falls into the pool of tears. The pool of tears becomes a sea, and as she swims there she meets a mouse. The mouse swims with Alice to the shore where they meet a group of animals on a bank. Alice spends some time with the animals but ends up scaring them away when she talks of her cat, Dinah.

Further on her journey, Alice comes upon the White Rabbit once more. He mistakes her for a servant and sends her to fetch his things within his house. She happens upon more substances, consuming a beverage that makes her grow to fill the house. The White Rabbit's servants throw rocks at her that magically turn into cakes. She eats one and shrinks down to normal size before making her escape.

Away from the White Rabbit's house, Alice comes across a smoking caterpillar. The caterpillar tells Alice of the different parts of the mushroom and how they can make her grow and shrink. They enter into an argument and the caterpillar leaves.

Wandering on, Alice comes to the duchess' house. It is full of characters including the Cheshire Cat. The duchess is holding her baby but wanting to get to the Queen's croquet game. She hands the baby over to Alice and leaves her. Alice looks down at the baby and realises it is a pig. She lets the pig go and leaves, again coming across the Cheshire Cat.

After telling her that everyone in Wonderland, including Alice herself, is completely mad the Cheshire Cat tells her where to find the March Hare's house.

Following the Cheshire Cat's directions, she comes to the March Hare's house to find herself part of a tea party with the Mad Hatter, the Doormouse and the March Hare. They are very rude to her and Alice discovers they are trapped in a never-ending tea time because they had 'crossed' Time. After too many insults, Alice departs.

She finds herself back in the great hall, drinks to shrink and opens the door to the coveted garden, this time prepared with the key.

Entering the garden, Alice comes upon three living playing cards painting the white roses on a rose tree red because The Queen of Hearts hates white roses. More cards, kings and queens, and even the White Rabbit, enter the garden. Alice then meets the King and Queen. The Queen, a figure difficult to please, introduces her signature phrase, 'Off with his head!' Which she utters at the slightest dissatisfaction with a subject. Alice is ordered to play a game of croquet with the Queen and the rest of her subjects. With the mallets being live flamingos and the balls reluctant hedgehogs, the game quickly becomes chaotic.

Alice once again meets the Cheshire Cat. The Queen of Hearts orders the Cat to be beheaded, only to have her executioner complain that this is impossible since the head is all that can be seen of him. Because the Cat belongs to the Duchess, the Queen is prompted to release the Duchess from gaol (whom she had previously imprisoned) to resolve the matter.

The Duchess tries to make friends with Alice but makes her feel uneasy. The Queen tells Alice she must meet the Mock Turtle and hear his story so she sends Alice off with the Gryphon. Meeting the Mock Turtle, they both share stories until they hear an announcement that the trial is about to begin. The Gryphon takes Alice back to the croquet garden.

The Knave of Hearts stands trial for having stolen the Queen's tarts. All of the characters from Wonderland give their nonsensical testimony and then Alice is called as a witness.

Suddenly a letter is produced that holds a poem, the King determines that this is an admission of guilt on behalf of the Knave. Alice is upset by the injustice and stands up for the Knave at which the Queen demands her execution.

The cards start to attack Alice. She fends them off for some time but they threaten to overwhelm her. Then her sister shakes her. She awakens lying in her sister's lap, her sister brushing leaves from her face.

THE JOURNEY AND RETURN IN OUR LIVES

The value in telling ourselves stories within this narrative structure is the growth that we expect to experience as a result of the discomfort we are facing whilst on the journey. We can embrace the hardship and the strangeness of what we are experiencing because we are anticipating development from this passage – development that will continue to serve us in our lives once this experience is complete.

Beware of this narrative because it has the potential of allowing one to fall into the passive – we may simply allow things to happen to us. We risk being a receiver of experiences with blind faith that it will help us grow, rather than taking active responsibility in shaping the experiences we are immersed in. We may also persist with something, convinced that the adversity has some higher purpose of personal growth for us. Whilst persistence is admirable, be sure that it is not futile!

The journey and return can be empowering if we are looking for ways to grow, develop and change ourselves in order to accommodate, or even succeed within, this new and unfamiliar world. If we want to be successful in our narration of our lives in the journey and return, be curious, open-minded and ready to learn. Although our circumstances may not change, we become better disposed to deal with them as a result of being on this journey.

The journey and return has many contextual applications (as do all the stories). Educational experiences, such as embarking on a course, have this application. Literal journeys also, when we travel into new places and experience the discomfort of being in a foreign place or embark on expeditions that herald difficulty, we can be served by considering these a journey and return narrative. We can accept being out of our comfort zone with the knowledge we will receive personal growth that will serve us both now and in the future as a return on our investment.

PART 3

The stories we tell ourselves

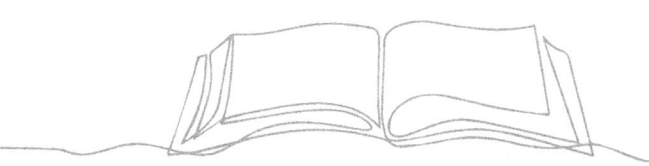

Here are our stories

This section of the book provides you with examples of stories from real life. These stories are inspired by the experiences of friends and family – stories that people have told me. I have given them fair warning: no story is sacred if they tell it to me!

There are stories in this section that reflect the lives of everyday lived experience as well as stories that are less common. I hope that within these stories you may find reflection of your own life experiences; some kind of connection with how your life has unfolded. You will be able to develop familiarity with the ways in which the seven stories can be applied to our life events, how we may construct our stories in a variety of ways, and how the different narratives can work in practice to serve us or otherwise.

You should also come to believe that no single storyline has more inherent value than any other. Each can serve or hinder equally depending on the circumstances, events and the characters involved.

Readers may also disagree with the perspectives of how these stories can help or hinder. That is fine! What is important is that you become familiar with the narrative patterns, develop competence in recognising them, are able to see how a person's story can be told in very different ways with different outcomes, and be able to identify the pathway forward we have within each narrative depending on the circumstances and the outcomes desired. The authenticity in the telling of the story, the way it works for *yourself* is the crux of this. YOU need to work out which narrative serves you when you tell your stories.

The initial section deals with stories where the narrative can be chosen in the moment. Further on, narratives will be illustrated to change over time. It is important for us to understand that a narrative that serves us right now may not have longevity. It may be that, over time, we need to change the way we narrate our stories so that the telling of stories to ourselves continues to be productive and serves us. This is all part of the process! The key thing is to be aware, reflective and apply a growth mindset. The rest will follow as we work toward recognising the pathway to living our best life.

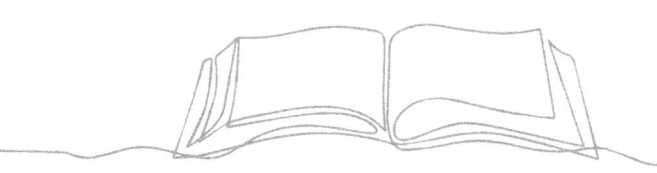

Public speaking – everybody's nightmare!

I surveyed the crowd to observe probably two or three hundred people. I felt a small leaping in my stomach and my palms were slightly sweaty. I thought to myself, this is okay, I know what I am going to say.

Then my name was called.

Suddenly, this moment was overwhelming. Standing in front of those people, I felt my mouth go dry. My heart raced and I could feel the pounding in my chest, my neck, my head. There was a resounding whooshing in my ears and, although I spoke to the crowd, I have no memory of what I said.

I experienced stage fright; a full blown panic attack in front of the audience.

Looking back, I realised that I probably had this anxiety for a long time. I just never recognised it as such. I knew I had to address this, so I embarked on a journey of self-development focusing on growing my skills and experience in the realm of public speaking.

Not content to remain in the small, supportive public speaking club environment that I had found with my local Toastmasters club, I determined that I would get on a bigger stage and really challenge myself.

In order to do this, I enlisted a fellow Toastmaster and together we founded a business we called Podium Public Speaking. We decided that as we both wanted more opportunities to speak on bigger stages and in more formal environments, we would create those opportunities for ourselves. So we did.

The team had worked exceptionally hard for eight weeks, developing speeches and organising the inaugural Podium Public Speaking event, *Finding Connection in a Digital World*. It was all coming together. However, I found myself losing my confidence. My anxiety kept building as the day loomed closer and I was not retaining my speech in my head in the way I had expected to. I was really pushing myself: I expected myself to go from a 5-7 minute Toastmasters speech to a 30 minute formal presentation. This was my monster and I was going to grow it! It came to a head eight days before the event when I had experienced a sleepless night and a migraine but had a dress rehearsal to attend that evening. I had a massive anxiety attack. I tried a glass of wine to calm my nerves, no luck there! I tried locking myself away and having a quick practice of my speech. Still the nerves were high. BUT, I pushed through and made myself speak during the dress rehearsal irrespective of how I was feeling.

I told myself, 'I have to do this. If I can speak feeling like this, I can do anything. I am just going to do it.'

My self-talk had me pitted against the monster but I was infusing myself with the strength to overcome it. I was equipping myself with the tools that I needed to defeat it.

I got through that rehearsal, although it was probably my worst ever performance! Then when it came to the actual event, I had that experience behind me which instilled in me a strength and a knowledge that, although this was big, I was going to do it. I was going to overcome the monster. I was nervous but I was prepared.

The day of the event finally arrived. Nervousness was the dish of the day but I told myself that it was healthy and worked to channel it into excitement. I did all the right things to keep my energies in check – practicing several times, some exercise, some meditation, visualisation of myself being successful and keeping myself busy on tasks that were not high pressure but at the same time all to do with making the night a success.

When I arrived at the venue I was able to remain very task oriented and then when the punters started to arrive, I really hit my stride. Talking to the audience members as they arrived kept my energies high and my last challenge was to sit in the theatre and wait my turn to speak. I was last on the bill – a long wait of one and a half hours!

Finally, my moment against the monster arrived but I was infused with excitement and ready to take it on. I had the time of my life, rolling through the prepared speech. I was interjecting humour as moments presented themselves, engaging with my audience, getting across my content. I really nailed that beast.

I came off the stage feeling a million dollars.

I AM NOT CINDERELLA!

Rags to riches: In a rags to riches narrative, we are unseen, overlooked, downtrodden and suffering. We have all the characteristics, skills and ability required to have all that we desire. But we are powerless to have these traits revealed. We have to work hard and stay true to ourselves.

If I was to consider the Cinderella story as my narrative, it would have me toiling away at the task of preparing for the event with a set of skills that I already had simply waiting to be revealed. Should I have seen myself as a Cinderella, I may not have devoted the effort required to have made the event and my speech as successful as it was. I would have been resting on my laurels, seeing myself as already having the skills and not working to grow them in order to be ready for this event. Should I have perceived my success due to a set of skills I already have on board, my success would have been shallower and basically ego-fulfilling. I doubt I would have been as good on stage and I certainly would not have experienced the rapture of my success.

I SLAYED THE MONSTER

Overcoming the monster: There is a conflict between us and something overwhelmingly big. We have to defeat this force that we see as monstrous and undefeatable.

The moment of tackling that public speaking event can be told as overcoming the monster. It was grown in my mind to be a beast. I felt overwhelmed. It was a big thing. However, during the preparation, I felt like I could acquire the skills and tools to defeat the beast. Treating this process as if I were overcoming the monster really served me. It did so because I convinced myself I had to work to acquire the skills to achieve what I intended. This is what I did. I practiced, I trained, I honed. When it came to the night I knew I had done my training; worked my "public speaking muscles". I was prepared. Whatever happened, I was going in to fight. I was as ready as I would ever be!

And when I was successful I had a peak experience – that perfect intersection of challenge and skills that left me feeling high for days. The opportunity to overcome a monster led me to believe I could now take on bigger monsters and still be successful. It has helped me grow as a person and develop my self-concept. I feel infinitely more capable as a result of this victory. The end result feels like a victory, an achievement, a success to be proud of. This narrative not only served me at the time but continues to be the narrative that has this life experience project its positivity into my future.

Waiting patiently in line… until!

Australians have very specific expectations around queueing. Anthony is just like any other Aussie in this regard. He and Jesla were queueing with Anna, their adult child, at the airport dutifully waiting their turn so they could farewell their daughter who was returning to Melbourne.

The queue was a nightmare. It snaked back and forth unendingly with what appeared to be thousands of people waiting to be checked in for their flight. Periodically, people for particular flights would be called forward as their departure time became too close to wait in line. This was acceptable to those in the queue.

However, the wait was oppressive. Finally, Anna's flight was the one for which people were being called forward.

The supervisor came forward. He opened one of the tabs that people arbitrarily follow when they are keeping to the rules of queueing. He then asked for the people flying on Anna's flight to step forward. This allowed a vast mob of people from the back of the queue to move forward; people who had just arrived, therefore, were given a queue jump in order to have their baggage checked and get into the departure lounge.

Anthony was incensed. So incensed that he acted out.

'Stop!' he shouted, addressing the crowd. He raised his hands in the air, attempting to prevent the tide of people from moving forward. And then he addressed the airline rep, 'We have all been waiting for ages for our check-in for the same flight and you are letting all these people through?'

'It's okay,' the company representative said. 'Everyone will get on the flight.'

Anthony was infuriated and created a fair amount of insurrection in the crowd as they waited, crankily this time, for their turn to be processed so they could wait some more in another location.

POOR LITTLE CINDERELLA

Rags to riches: In a rags to riches narrative, we are unseen, overlooked, downtrodden and suffering. We have all the characteristics, skills and ability required to have all that we desire. But we are powerless to have these traits revealed. We have to work hard and stay true to ourselves.

Initially, Anthony was waiting in the line, doing his duty. The wait was oppressive and he was accepting that some circumstances called for queue jumping. However, he undertook that with reasonable humour because his turn would come in due course and his hard graft would be rewarded. When the story didn't play out as he believed it should, where he would get his turn justly, he was angry. He tried to rectify the situation, to have the good qualities that he and the others waiting in line had shown recognised and rewarded.

This did not occur. And when Anthony was not rewarded for his good behaviour, Anthony was not a happy camper. So long as the reward was his in due course, he would have been satisfied. However, in the absence of this reward, the rags to riches narrative could not serve Anthony.

COULD HE SEE THE HUMOUR?

Comedy: There is confusion obscuring the truth. It creates problems and misunderstandings as a result.

Neither Anthony or the airline official understood each other's position. Anthony tried to have his thoughts heard. When Anthony spoke up to put forward his point of view but the airline representative then gave his own viewpoint contrary to Anthony's, this story had the potential for having confusion cleared up and acceptance of the situation as a happy ending. Anthony, though, did not accept the other man's point of view. The official also had no interest in Anthony's viewpoint. Although there was no longer confusion, things went ahead as the official decreed. This only served to infuriate Anthony further.

Another narrative that did not help Anthony.

ANTHONY TOOK ON THE MONSTER

Overcoming the monster: There is a conflict between us and something overwhelmingly big. We have to defeat this force that we see as monstrous and undefeatable.

Not accepting the circumstances, building the overbearing wait into something intolerable and then seeing the people from the back of the queue brought forward as unjust, all helped Anthony to shape this situation as a monster to be overcome. He attempted to take on the monster and to fight the injustice. His tool was logic and he tried to argue for all those waiting with him.

He was unsuccessful. He lost and this made him cranky. Others also tapped into that feeling and the crowd was quite dissatisfied.

Telling this narrative as overcoming the monster grew the anger and frustration because this monster was not able to be defeated.

MOURN THE LOSS OF JUSTICE

Tragedy: The situation or characters involved are fundamentally flawed. The flaws create continual issues and get in the way of any successful outcome. The tragedy needs to be accepted, loss mourned and the characters need to move on.

Unless they felt a full scale riot was called for to restore the expected order of things, at some point Anthony, his companions and the others waiting with them would need to accept the circumstances. To be able to move on with their lives and not hold on to the anger that sits within them as a result of this situation, they would need to see the whole thing as unresolvable, mourn its loss and put it to bed. If they could take a moment to breathe, to let go of the anger they held inside, they may have been able to apply the tragedy narrative and accept their circumstances. Holding on to the anger about the situation would only serve to cause self-injury and unhappiness. It certainly wouldn't serve them, unless they have a pathway to right this injustice.

A NEW QUEST

The quest: There is a greater goal we are seeking. We face distractions and challenges along the way to achieving this goal which contribute to the learning and growth we require; growing our capacity to achieve the bigger goal. We have help along the way and we expect this to be a lengthy commitment.

If Anthony could not let this go, he may choose to use channels for complaint and make this his pursuit. If he truly believed some kind of compensation was in order for having had the long wait and been 'queue jumped' he may well pursue this.

This may help him in the short term to be able to cope with his circumstances. If he could take a moment to consider this potential pathway to justice, he may be able to feel empowered in his narrative and be satisfied that a resolution will come.

However, when we step back from the event and look at the bare bones of what happened, he was annoyed – perhaps there was some pain and suffering; in that – but there was no financial loss incurred and his daughter caught her scheduled flight. He may be barking up the wrong tree and again following a narrative that doesn't serve him. As a way to get through his heightened emotions in the moment, this narrative may have been useful, long term, he probably would need to return to the tragedy and just let it go!

A PATH TO DISCOVERY?

Journey and return: Our world is changed or is in some way unfamiliar, causing discomfort. We need to acquire new learning and adjust in order to succeed.

Anthony was enduring unpleasant circumstances while waiting in the queue. But when the man opened up the section to let the queue jumpers through, he was plunged into an unfamiliar world. In the journey and return, the protagonist needs to look inside themselves and experience some kind of internal change or new level of understanding in order to cope with this new world.

So long as Anthony understood that his daughter was not going to miss her flight, reaching inside and finding a new level of patience taught to him by this unfamiliar world where people did things differently to what he expected may also have served to help him cope with this unfortunate situation he had found himself in. For him to be able to let his emotions go in the moment he may need to harness some breathing techniques. Perhaps add in some kind of positive self-talk, telling himself, "We get to spend more time together before she has to go through the gate." Or an affirmation: "It's OK, she will get her flight." These can help Anthony to accept the narrative told in the form of the journey and return and simply enjoy the last moments he had with his daughter before she stepped on the plane and flew thousands of kilometres away.

Angela goes hard

I have engaged in many physically arduous events. The Busselton Ironman 70.3, the Augusta Adventure Race, the Perth Marathon are just some examples.

The 70.3 involves a 1.9 km swim, 90 km bike ride and a 21.1 km run. The Adventure Race was a 13.5 km run, 13 km paddle, 1.9 km swim, 32 km mountain bike ride and a second run of 3.5 km. They were pretty full on tasks. And the marathon was a 42.2 km run. Interestingly, although the other events were longer, the marathon was more challenging for me as it only had one 'leg' of such length.

Anyone who has competed in these events (for me I use the word, 'competed' loosely. This girl here is an 'also ran'!) knows that race day is but one part of the whole process.

The significant part of these events is the preparation and readiness.

When I trained for the marathon, my training began months prior. I took advice and planned my training schedule so that I built up to a thirty-five kilometre run in my peak training week before the event. I had to keep my body healthy. This meant regular massages, visits to a podiatrist for dry needling, lots of taping and significant deep water running. Training for the marathon took away all the healthy cross training I had undertaken for the other events I had done and put lots of stress on my body! I also focused on diet, making sure I was fuelling my body well and choosing healthy carbs for the process of carb loading before big runs. I recall a conversation with a guy called Junky at my friend, Sandy's, birthday bash. We were sat next to each other. He was a seasoned marathon runner and I was a newbie. He gave me lots of advice about nutrition during the race. My friend, Clive, was also very helpful as an experienced runner. Now there's a guy who has chalked up some extended and arduous feats! He told me how he used carb jubes to fuel himself during the race. This appealed to me, a little reward every so often to keep me going. Thanks, Clive! It was great to take advice from those with experience.

I remember some of the training was pretty tough. The marathon was a winter event, which could have been awful but turned out perfect. However, the greater training was during the lead up to the end of autumn and coming into winter. There were days of quite hideous storms but the training waits for no-one. If I was going to be prepared for the marathon I needed to train. I worked during the day and knew my best energy was always in the morning, so I would be doing two to three hours of run training prior to school (I worked as a teacher) at least once a week in addition to shorter sessions. Often, I trained for the first hour in darkness. Our road is a circle of one kilometre in length so I would do about twelve laps of the circle before venturing further when the sun came up. I was a bit nervous running further afield in the dark! One day the weather was abysmal and I put off my morning run. But the weather just never got better all day. I couldn't bring myself to run out in those conditions, so I dragged my butt to the gym and got on the treadmill. People came and went; I chatted away with a few people. The RPM group fitness classes took place in the same gym room. The participants faced away from me and the treadmill away from them. They came and went, interacting with the back of my head during this training session. Two hours on the treadmill! Thank goodness for all the interaction because it was still the toughest training I had ever done, even tougher than the road run I did later on that was almost twice the length.

Oh and did I mention I am not a runner? I have never considered myself a runner. I think of myself as such even less now, but there I was, plugging away!

Until I trained for the marathon my longest run was 21.1 km. In training I ran that so many times and beyond that I lost count. My brother in law often quipped, 'the tyranny of the long distance runner.' I am not quite sure what that meant, but because I am not a runner and each big run is certainly tyrannous in some respect, it felt right.

Finally race day came. I got a lift to the start line with a kind soul who was also taking part. However, Michael was going to be finished well before me so I made sure someone else was ready to take me home! I was my usual nervy self, had a few nervous toilet breaks before the beginning but finally the start horn blew and we were underway. I always settle once the race commences.

Things started off quite well. We had a very picturesque run beside the Swan River for a long time. I managed to be running alongside the same lady for ages, so we got to talking and that helped to pass the time. Eventually she stopped at a drink station and I continued on. We never crossed paths again, I never even found out her name.

I had some mantras that were working for me, like, 'if you don't jog it, you can't log it.' Basically, I decided that I needed to keep moving forward. I would take hydration from the hydration stations but would remain on the move, 'If you walk it you can't chalk it.' I convinced myself that unless I kept moving at a gait that resembled jogging or running, it didn't count and thus I kept going. At about the 32 km mark I saw my friend, Jenny, and her girls. I was stoked to see her there; it gave me such a lift so long into the run to have their friendly faces cheering me on.

The last 7 km were the hardest. They were the kilometres beyond what I had done in my training and lord I felt every one of them. I hammered out my mantras and pressed forward. Thank goodness for the lovely environment and the cheering crowds. These all pushed me along in the task. And eventually those kilometres were done. I crossed the finish line, got my shirt and hugged my family.

I was done.

A REBIRTH

Rebirth: There is a problem within ourselves that necessitates change or learning in order to resolve the conflict in our lives.

I could tell this story to myself as a rebirth. I had certainly effected a change, and needed to! I had to look at myself, auditing how I was doing prior to commencing training and set a training program that would turn a non-runner into a marathon runner. This was a success and I achieved the completion of a marathon because of what I became. This narrative could serve me. However, I did not maintain the capacity to run a marathon. In fact, I have done very little running since, so I can't truly say I am rebirthed as a runner! I am not sure that this narrative quite fits as something to look back on and have impact my life positively going forward. When I visualise this, something is missing in telling my narrative this way.

MY LONG QUEST

The quest: There is a greater goal we are seeking. We face distractions and challenges along the way to achieving this goal which contribute to the learning and growth we require; growing our capacity to achieve the bigger goal. We have help along the way and we expect this to be a lengthy commitment.

I could see this marathon as a quest and this narrative would serve me well. The actual event, the marathon itself, was the overarching goal. But leading up to that were so many challenges: long runs, sore legs, bad weather. I had many people giving me advice – my sidekicks – leading up to the event and some on the day as well. I could break down the training into chunks and then even break down the event itself into pieces in order to get it done. I had my magical spells by way of mantras to keep me running through the pain. Seeing it as a quest definitely serves me. To be able to take the quest one challenge at a time really helps when there is a long path to that bigger goal. It helps to visualise the achievement of the small steps and count those small wins along the way as I build the skills and capacity to achieve that final big run.

A JOURNEY AND RETURN

Journey and return: Our world is changed or is in some way unfamiliar, causing discomfort. We need to acquire new learning and adjust in order to succeed.

During post-event reflections I can visualise this marathon 'era' as a journey and return. I embarked on a journey in 'unfamiliar territory', being a non-runner entering the runner's world. I did have to find some kind of transformation within myself in order to be able to deal with this new world as a runner and grow into the person who made the distance in the marathon event. And although I did not continue to be a runner when the event ended, I have developed from the experience and have a level of resilience and capacity to overcome that I did not have before because of having gone on this journey. I think this is a narrative that continues to serve me after the marathon has faded into the past. And when I tell the narrative in this way, I still have the experience and the growth of having achieved this mammoth journey to call upon in my life when things get tough. I have learnt how to dig deep for sure!

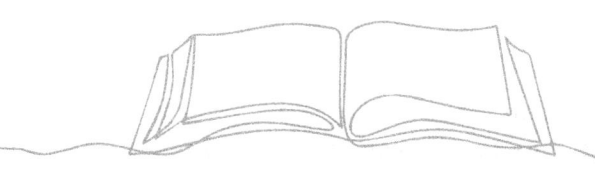

A challenging adventure in a natural wonderland

Tommo is an outdoor education teacher. He takes students on all manner of adventures and has many stories to tell.

A favourite expedition of his is a trip to the Shark Bay region of Western Australia. The environment is wild and harsh yet striking in its beauty. The vivid red sand contrasts with the cerulean blue sky and the teals and jades of the water.

Even the wildlife inspires awe – dugongs, dolphins, turtles, sea snakes, and more frightening creatures such as stone fish, sharks and cone snails. It is an environment of immense beauty and incredible contrasts.

The weather also shows extremes. It can often be exceptionally hot and it rarely rains. Sometimes the weather is exquisitely still, other times the winds are merciless.

The expedition Tommo takes students on is an extended paddle. They spend three nights and four days in this wilderness, packing all of their requirements into kayaks and paddling seventy-something kilometres of the coastline in an out-and-back journey.

Although the expedition is well-supported with vehicles and support boats, the participants have every sense of being isolated and self-sufficient. All of their requirements must be carried by themselves; the support vehicles do not carry for them. Students pit themselves against themselves and against the elements.

After a trip of nine hundred kilometres, including an overnight stay in the quirky caravan park in the old telegraph station of Hamelin Pool, the group arrives in Denham. The mammoth task of unloading their gear and stuffing their requisites for three nights and four days into a kayak they share with a buddy commences. Tommo gives non-committal responses to the students as they work through what they need and what they must do themselves.

Eventually this work is done and the students embark upon the first stages of their journey.

Things start beautifully. With a delightful tail wind, the journey goes relatively easily and the students build their paddling fitness. They wonder at the environment and to their delight witness dugongs eating the seagrasses, large turtles swimming by and dolphins fishing. There is no rush as they paddle gently through the still waters, stopping occasionally for a dip and for a drink of water. Lunch is eaten on a pristine beach. The only footprints other than those of the group seem to be from birds and lizards. Such a privilege for these kids to be able to have this wilderness experience.

Mirth erupts from most of the group members at one point. A male student is sharing a kayak with his girlfriend. He has the rear of the craft and she sits in the front. He decides to stand on the kayak in order to take a leak. Things are going along well until he suddenly overbalances, taking himself and his girlfriend into the water, along with much of their once dry (but no longer) sleeping gear! Whilst the rest of the group are rolling around at the humour of the situation, his girlfriend does not share their sense of fun and rides him mercilessly for some time about his carelessness and the fact that she will be having an uncomfortable sleep that night with her wet pillow and sleeping bag!

Eventually the group reach the intended campsite and set up. They have their dinner, almost everyone having prepared noodles, complete their debrief and then hit the sack early intending to be up and at 'em early the next day.

And so things go on this trip; more beautiful blue sky, more clear aquamarine water, more amazing sea life, more delightful swims. And then it is time for the return journey.

The breeze is against them on the way back. On the second to last day, the breeze is notable but not overwhelming. The group feel like they have the wherewithal to cope with what the day throws at them.

On the last day the group is tired. They have existed on a diet of noodles and mountain bread. They want tasty food; want to slake their thirst with something other than water; want their own bed and their own pillow. They are getting tired. To add insult to injury, the head wind decides to pick up. What was doable the day before now seems infinitely more vast.

But these are great kids and they are committed to the journey, so they pack up their kayaks and prepare themselves for the long day ahead. Twenty-two kilometres until they could consider themselves done.

The group start paddling. The wind howls into their faces and ebbs away at their strength. This wonderland starts to develop into a nightmare. The kids are losing their strength and eventually they come to a stop.

'We can't do this, Tommo. There is no way. It is just too hard,' they say in one voice.

Tommo calls them over and insists they take a break. He brings the group together and offers them his wise counsel as a seasoned expeditioner, 'Yes, you *can* do it. You can. What you are trying to do is too big in one step.'

He offers them a strategy for success: 'Break it down into smaller steps. Go a kilometre, have a rest, go another kilometre and have a rest. It is hard, but you can do it.' They have ten kilometres to go.

The group starts paddling again. Tommo expects a break in a kilometre, but the group doesn't stop. They keep going. And going. And going. And they paddle all the way through to the end.

They make it, tired but happy.

At the debrief they say if Tommo hadn't given them the talk they wouldn't have made it. And they speak of that camp for a very long time thereafter. Every one of those kids emerges from the camp stronger – better – with more drive and more resilience because they face adversity and they push through.

VERY NEARLY A TRAGEDY

Tragedy: The situation or characters involved are fundamentally flawed. The flaws create continual issues and get in the way of any successful outcome. The tragedy needs to be accepted, loss mourned and the characters need to move on.

The kids on this adventure were spent. They were ready to give up on the undertaking. They wanted out, wanted to call it quits. But they had worked so hard and to quit now, they would always carry that failure with them. They just didn't know how they could keep going. Tommo wasn't going to let this pan out as a tragedy. He knew that if they stopped then, they would have lost the opportunity to push through and grow from the experience. He was not going to let them let themselves down. He rallied the troops and kept them going. He helped them to shift their narrative away from this potential tragedy.

A COMEDY?

Comedy: There is confusion obscuring the truth. It creates problems and misunderstandings as a result.

It is true that these kids did not see the truth of what they were capable of in that moment. They had had a great time until that last day but then felt spent. They did not realise that they could keep going. This loss of their own truth was potentially holding them back. However, being told they can do something and knowing they can are two different animals. Is this the most relevant representation of the story? Is this the story that would serve them? I don't believe the comedy had the power to shift the thinking of these kids at the time to a belief that they could press on.

JOURNEY AND RETURN

Journey and return: Our world is changed or is in some way unfamiliar, causing discomfort. We need to acquire new learning and adjust in order to succeed.

The group were certainly in an unfamiliar environment. They were initially in that dream state where everything seemed fine and they were enjoying the points of difference between their home world and this magical natural wonderland. However, at some point the environment became uncomfortable enough to tip them out of their comfort zone. These kids needed to find something inside themselves, to effect some change that would then help them to survive/succeed in this new environment, a change that would be taken home with them and improve their lives thereafter. Tommo's pep talk and offering of a new strategy was able to get the participants to dig deep and find the change in themselves that they needed for this narrative to see itself to a positive conclusion. Isn't it curious that they didn't even follow the strategy suggested and yet they found it within themselves to make it to the end?! Fortunately for the kids on the expedition, they had a guide to help them realise they had it in themselves to make it through. If the students were aware of this telling and had the ability to look at their narrative from the outside, then they may well have been able to effect this change themselves. Maybe, going forward, this experience will have offered that to them. They may have that capacity in the future as a result. Either way, the journey and return is a narrative that served this group of adventurers. To recognise they were in discomfort, and they had the power within themselves to overcome, was key to their success. They grew as a result of this journey, which aided them in completing the journey itself and allowed them to become better, stronger people in their lives once they returned. Which is an added beauty of the journey and return narrative, it can continue to serve us as we move into our futures.

A loving mother

Folding the fabric, she released a jet of steam from the iron to ensure the crease was permanent. She admired the softness of the cotton and the pretty pink flowers and thought of the baby girl who would be wrapped in this beautiful handmade gift she was crafting. Inevitably this turned her thoughts to her own family. She wondered if she would ever feel the softness of the baby skin of her own grandchildren one day. To smell their milky scent, to breathe them in and have that feeling of love brim and threaten to overwhelm as she stared down into their downy, sleepy heads.

She feared she never would.

Sandy is a wonderful mother and a truly giving human being. She was the active parent when her boys were little (now grown up). She was the one who dealt with their scrapes, fed them and bathed them, organised their school lives and their social lives, took them to sports. She was the one who taught them to throw and catch and took them out to practice. She was the one who provided for all of their needs.

Sandy's husband was much less involved. He directed the world grumpily from his easy chair. The family knew well enough when they had 'got it wrong' but he wasn't one for praise or demonstrations of love. That was Sandy's department.

The marriage lasted decades, and then it didn't. Sandy gave and gave to this loveless man. Finally she had decided, after enduring this marriage for way too long, that it was over. Sandy had waited until the boys were old enough and finally ended it. She told the family and moved on with her life.

Her now ex-husband did not take it well. He was shocked; surprised indeed that she was unhappy and would want to leave. He shaped her as a wrongdoer and adversely influenced her boys to feel the same way. The boys stopped seeing their mum.

It has been many years since Sandy has seen her much-loved children. Every now and then she reaches out, makes sure they know the door is open. She has been repeatedly rebuffed. She keeps tabs on them, aware of where they are, so that she can rekindle the relationship when they are ready.

Tears fall on the whimsical fabric as she contemplates a future where she never holds her children or grandchildren. But she still lives in hope.

ISN'T THIS SITUATION MONSTROUS?

Overcoming the monster: There is a conflict between us and something overwhelmingly big. We have to defeat this force that we see as monstrous and undefeatable.

Sandy's husband certainly fit the bill as a monster and the situation itself was monstrous too. It is big; it is ugly. It would be an easy thing for Sandy to take this situation on as a stoush. And she would have to; the pathway forward in the overcoming the monster narrative is to take that monster on. She could be angry and rail against the situation. It may work if she is willing to take on the fight, to argue with her ex, to fight for – or even with – her boys about the situation. Maybe they want that?

Sandy would need to be prepared to invest a lot of angry emotion and energy into the situation and it may not work in her favour. The possibility exists that she would end up in a worse situation that she is in now and any 'fighting' she does could result in affirming the negative opinions held of her.

In any situation where a fight takes place, there will be a winner and a loser. If she tells this narrative as an overcoming the monster narrative, and takes on the fight, she may end up the loser.

Alternatively, they may respond disinterestedly. The rebuffing she has experienced previously could occur, in fact this is a highly likely scenario. This is very hurtful to Sandy and, as humans, we are wired to seek pleasure and move away from pain. She is unlikely to want to seek this scenario, for good reason.

It is hard to see how telling this story as an overcoming the monster, where the only pathway forward is to fight, is going to serve Sandy.

IS THIS ACTUALLY A TRAGEDY?

Tragedy: The situation or characters involved are fundamentally flawed. The flaws create continual issues and get in the way of any successful outcome. The tragedy needs to be accepted, loss mourned and the characters need to move on.

What an awful situation. My heart bleeds for this beautiful lady and the loss of her relationship with her children. I hate seeing the pain this causes her and wish for her that it did not exist. A loving parent deserves a loving relationship with their children.

While this is a very sad state of affairs, a devoted mother estranged from her children, it would be devastating to think that this is the end of the road for the family. An absolutely heartbreaking situation to consider a life where she will never see her boys again. Without the hope of seeing her children again someday, Sandy would find life untenable and the grief unbearable. Visualising this narrative gives rise to terrible feelings of loss. Should she narrate the events as a tragedy, Sandy would be trapped in the nightmare stage of the narrative, forever in a state of grief. This would not serve Sandy.

WHAT IF SHE CHANGED?

Rebirth: There is a problem within ourselves that necessitates change or learning in order to resolve the conflict in our lives.

Sandy could look at herself and try to find some way to change, to be a better person, a more caring mother. She could take action and change herself.

However, in this circumstance, this is not going to be the best course of action.

This is not a situation where Sandy can look inside herself and find some kind of opportunity to change internally in order to be accepted by her children. She already gave everything she had to motherhood and did a bang-up job. Her children have had their opinion of their mother changed by someone toxic. They are not even seeing her, let alone seeing any effort she would be putting into self-improvement. To work on herself for her children would be fruitless and probably soul destroying. (To work on herself for *herself*, of course, would ALWAYS be good!)

IF ONLY THEY COULD SEE HER

Rags to riches: In a rags to riches narrative, we are unseen, overlooked, downtrodden and suffering. We have all the characteristics, skills and ability required to have all that we desire. But we are powerless to have these traits revealed. We have to work hard and stay true to ourselves.

This can be told as a rags to riches story.

Sandy has all the wonderful qualities of being a good mother that simply need to be recognised and rewarded. She is living under the tyranny of a toxic ex-husband who is poisoning her boys against her. Perhaps, if she is patient and continues to keep the opportunity for reconnection available to her children they will eventually come around; see their father for who he is and see Sandy for the person she is – a wonderful, loving mother who gave them everything and withstood an awful marriage in order to give them the best she could for as long as she could. Maybe when they are older and wiser, perhaps have children of their own, they will be ready to reunite.

This way of telling the narrative to herself serves in that it keeps hope alive. As humans age, we often develop wisdoms that elude the young and having children of our own is a profoundly life-changing experience. It is worth thinking that these events could bring her children to their senses.

In a situation where taking a proactive role is not really available to us, continuing to be a good person, making sure we remain aligned with our values, putting up with some injustice or unfairness with the hope that things will change and our qualities will be revealed resulting in us getting our reward, can genuinely be the best course of action. That is likely here.

For Sandy to be able to be patient and accepting of her circumstances in this narrative she may apply some affirmations, such as, "I am a good person and I am worthy of good things," or, "I am honourable and good things will come to me." If she can maintain her positive self-belief, this narrative can serve her.

Chasing the title of 'best bowler'

Marcus has been working hard on his bowling. His dad takes him down to the nets quite regularly where he bowls a stack of balls, practicing his technique and trying to improve.

He walks away from the crease with the ball in his hand. He spins the ball in his fingers to settle his nerves. He finds the mark, the spot where he needs to turn around and commence his run up. He thinks about the batter, where they have been hitting lately and what their weaknesses are so he can bowl to their deficits. He starts walking and develops into a jog. He holds the ball in both hands, spinning it with his right hand and palming it with his left. He gets close to the crease and he looks at the spot where he wants to bowl. The ball is in his right hand now. He lifts his arm up and brings it around in an arc. He spins the ball left with two fingers and his thumb kicks it out as he releases the ball, driving it forward into a spin. Marcus stops running and watches the batsman to see where he moves to, anticipating the shot and preparing himself to field.

In practice, he finds that he will bowl the first balls really well, but then he starts to overthink and things go awry. He will bowl all over the place and he starts to talk negatively to himself, playing the 'blame game' – blaming the wind, his sore arm or leg, the surface.

After a while he catches himself in his negative thinking. He reframes. He gives himself a clean slate, forgetting all the bad balls that have come before this one he is about to bowl. He tells himself he is capable, that he can and has achieved good bowls under these conditions. Marcus asks for and listens to advice about his technique. He keeps bowling and always likes to finish on a good bowl.

He also sets smaller goals for himself. His current short-term goal is to keep a positive mindset. His medium-term goal is to bowl well under all conditions, maintaining his high average of good balls in all conditions.

Marcus recognises that he needs to put more effort in to his practice bowling, he really seems to lift on game day and tends to be a bit lazy in the nets. His percentage of good bowls in practice is about 60% compared to a game-day average of 80%.

All of this is working toward his goal of being able to bowl well in any conditions and to be the best bowler in his team. When pressed as to what that means he says, 'The one who gets the most wickets.'

HE IS NO CINDERS

Rags to riches: In a rags to riches narrative, we are unseen, overlooked, downtrodden and suffering. We have all the characteristics, skills and ability required to have all that we desire. But we are powerless to have these traits revealed. We have to work hard and stay true to ourselves.

If Marcus was to frame his bowling skill in the rags to riches narrative, he would not have to do anything except keep bowling and wait for others to recognise how good he is.

Marcus is not waiting to have his current skill set revealed. The Cinderella story does not serve Marcus on a journey of self-improvement because there is no commitment to improvement, simply an expectation that people will realise he is already good. Marcus recognises that he has work to do in order to improve his bowling and achieve his goal.

REBORN AS A MASTER BOWLER?

Rebirth: There is a problem within ourselves that necessitates change or learning in order to resolve the conflict in our lives.

A rebirth would see Marcus transform himself internally, to look inside and make changes to himself in order to be the better bowler.

But this is only part of the story. Should Marcus tell himself this narrative as a rebirth, he would be dealing with his internal monologue but denying the physical practice he needs to undertake and the support of others required in order to up his skill level and consistency.

MARCUS IS DETERMINED TO GET HIS GOAL

The quest: There is a greater goal we are seeking. We face distractions and challenges along the way to achieving this goal which contribute to the learning and growth we require; growing our capacity to achieve the bigger goal. We have help along the way and we expect this to be a lengthy commitment.

Marcus has set himself up with a quest. He has a long-term goal of being the best bowler and he has broken it down into smaller challenges. He knows this is a long journey and he will need to put in a significant commitment to achieve his goal. He takes advice from a team of people to develop further.

This really works for Marcus as he commits to applying himself over and over to the work he needs to do in order to achieve his short, medium and long term goals.

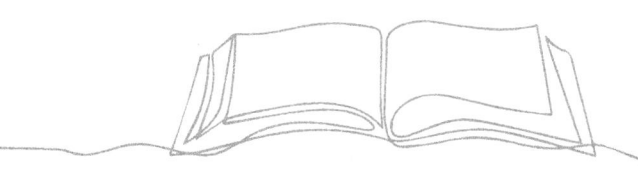

A suicidal teen

The girl wipes her tears as she admires the gleaming blade of the knife. She doesn't understand why but she knows that the pain of the knife slicing through her porcelain flesh negates the pain wrenching her soul. She lines the blade up so it makes a vertical line running an absolute perfect parallel to those that already stripe her inner arm. Pulling the blade across her skin, she sees the blood well in the cut and feels a calm pervade her body, if only for a minute, taking away this entrenched agony of her daily existence. She allows crimson to drip onto the basin and enjoys that fleeting sense of well-being that she seems to only get from assaulting her flesh.

...

Peta rearranged the roses in the vase for the umpteenth time, just trying to get them right, and bent to smell them. She wiped the table once more and then rinsed the cloth before turning her attention to the bathroom. After spraying the cleanser around the shower recess she grabbed the cloth ready to clean the basin. It was then she noticed some unexpected stains on the bench. Tucking her long, blonde hair behind her ear, she bent for a closer inspection. Blood! Her pulse quickened in fear. In her family, the presence of blood on the basin is rarely an innocent accident.

Taking some deep breaths to calm herself, not knowing what she was about to encounter, Peta walked to her daughter's closed bedroom door. She rapped gently and opened the door with a trembling fist to see her daughter's face staring accusingly back at her, hatred seeming to burn from her scrutinising face. The words that spewed forth from her child's mouth were bitter and contemptuous. And post-tirade, the child grabbed a bag of clothes together, announcing she was leaving.

Peta felt helpless. Her beautiful 16-year-old daughter was the source of constant turmoil and worry in Peta's world. This girl is supermodel gorgeous. She is smart. But she is in trouble. She is struggling. When this girl looks in the mirror, she fails to see the beauty apparent to everyone else's observation. She does not see any value in herself. Her gaze is one of self-hatred and she turns this hatred outwardly on those close to her. And quickly a peaceful moment in the household becomes a warzone because of the child's inner chaos. But the more she tries to help her, the more the child pulls away. It only seems to grow the anger and resentment.

Peta watched her child, dressed in long sleeves despite the heat, exit the house muttering angrily and wondered when and if she would see her again. Her recent self-harm and suicide attempts have been horrific for Peta and the actively venomous way in which her child refuses Peta's kindness and help leaves the woman feeling even more helpless to intervene, to parent, to give love.

Peta made herself a green tea and sat, placing her hand on her forehead. She felt such guilt over the place her daughter was in. Her daughter had really struggled since Peta broke up with Steve, the father of her children and her husband for 23 years. Although Peta and Steve were amicable and cared for one another as friends, the children were having to deal with change they did not choose. They were split across households, spending some of their time at Mum's and some at Dad's. Their son seemed to accept his circumstances with equanimity but their daughter didn't feel like she truly belonged anywhere. She wanted her old life back and everything felt wrong; off-kilter. She felt helpless and like her life was completely out of control. And she blamed everyone, seeing the break up as the source of her pain and her mum as ground zero.

Peta was very frustrated, in her own agony, and desperate for a way forward.

COULD THIS BE A TRAGEDY?

Tragedy: The situation or characters involved are fundamentally flawed. The flaws create continual issues and get in the way of any successful outcome. The tragedy needs to be accepted, loss mourned and the characters need to move on.

To perceive this story as a tragedy, Peta would need to either see her daughter as flawed and never able to grow beyond the experience she is currently in, or to see this situation as something she simply cannot resolve. This would involve an acceptance of the way things are, an opportunity to mourn what has been lost, her happy-go-lucky, loving daughter, and to move on with her life.

Although there have been some pretty horrific times for the family as her daughter deals with her torrid emotions and the family experience the fallout, this story is by no means finished. And Peta is not quite ready to give up. If Peta were to write her daughter off, she would feel very guilty, she would become trapped in the nightmare of grief and loss and wonder if there were not more she could do. No way could this devoted mother give up on her daughter so soon. She is very invested in trying to find resolution to the ongoing nightmare of her daughter's mental health situation. If it were to be written off as a tragedy, she could lose this beautiful girl. The tragedy narrative in no way serves Peta or her daughter at the moment. Let's hope it never comes to that. They need to see this as still having the potential for improvement and keep putting the work in. There is hope!

CONVICTION IN REBIRTH

Rebirth: There is a problem within ourselves that necessitates change or learning in order to resolve the conflict in our lives.

I find this whole thing incredibly difficult. My heart breaks and I am also incredibly afraid. I couldn't bear it if something happened to my girl. But she will find change within herself. She will find strength. She will find beauty. She will find her path. This is a transition phase. Her life is hard at the moment, but she is getting all the right help. She is my butterfly. I really think this will be her year.

When Peta frames this story as a rebirth, she sees her daughter as able to experience the change required in order to experience better mental health, to restore her to the girl she was or could be and to rebuild their relationship. Peta can have the belief that her daughter will experience a change that is going to make everything better. Perceiving the situation in this frame has her seeing this situation as temporary and she can look to putting the supports in place to drive that catalyst to change that she knows is required and she believes will occur. This is very positive and empowering. The challenge in framing the story as a rebirth, however, is that it is not Peta who is needing to change, it is her daughter. Peta needs to be mindful of her daughter's feelings and experience, and give her the space and time to effect her own rebirth. If she tries to force this along, then she may find that she becomes very frustrated with the whole thing. She can see what needs to happen, but this isn't *her* story of rebirth, it is her daughter's. She will need to allow her daughter to hold that space and to tell her own story. She will have to exercise much patience in narrating this story to herself as a rebirth. All she can do is lay out the path for her daughter and let her walk her own way.

Peta can reflect on her telling of the story and if the rebirth narrative is losing its ability to generate faith in a positive action, if it no longer serves her to feel like she is in control of her life and able to steer this as she wants to, turning to the hero's journey, or the quest, is a useful course of action.

ANOTHER EPIC?

The quest: There is a greater goal we are seeking. We face distractions and challenges along the way to achieving this goal which contribute to the learning and growth we require; growing our capacity to achieve the bigger goal. We have help along the way and we expect this to be a lengthy commitment.

The quest is such a great fall-back narrative. It allows us to expect the long haul and many events along the way: hiccups through to massive challenges that help us to grow into the capacity to overcome the greater, overarching challenge. But it won't all be bad, there will be periods of respite where everything seems okay, and there will be times where significant challenges arise. When we are thinking of its application here, this is all on that long journey toward the prize of mental health. It is important for Peta and her daughter to remember that in the journey, the hero has many people to call on who can assist, people whose strengths and skills are diverse and they have a broad range of things to offer in order to overcome challenges. Seek help!

This narrative can fit quite well in the telling of the story and can actually serve to help Peta and her daughter deal with the trials and tribulations of seeking mental wellness. Peta's daughter has had many challenges as her story unfolds. There have been periods of respite where she is feeling okay, where things seem to have calmed for the family, however, the quest is far from over. Simply knowing that there will be periods of high stress and challenge followed by periods of respite can be reassuring in itself. Knowing that this is a long journey and not a sprint helps to set them up for this rather than the expectation that getting through one drama means they have completed the journey only to fall back into the next drama on the path.

In addition, Peta and her daughter need to be sure to call on professional help, the support of family and friends, the support of each other. But, again, Peta needs to be mindful of imposing help. In these situations, we need to remember to tell our own story and not someone else's. It is highly likely that if Peta overtly imposes her belief in a certain course of action on her daughter, this may be rejected – she is a teenager who may need to find her own way. It will require careful parenting and strategic communication and plan for support for Peta to have her daughter adopt a wise course of action. Other voices, voices other than a parent.

Wise counsellors are very useful in achieving this level of support required.

The risks within the quest narrative is that the expectation of ordeals may be established and therefore become self-fulfilling and the lack of resilience for the long and arduous journey may make it too hard to deal with. In adopting the quest as our narrative we need to make this preparation.

Patience!

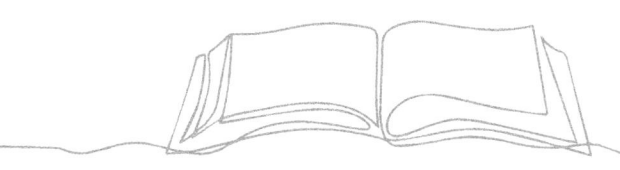

Angela jumps out of a perfectly good aeroplane

When I was in my twenties, I decided I needed to jump out of a perfectly good aeroplane. I was hanging around with some pretty adventurous types in a martial arts gym and we made this our new challenge. We enrolled in a course with the aim of completing a static line jump from an aircraft. This type of jump has the parachute attached to the plane by a line that automatically pulls the chute for the jumper. But they are on their own up there. The easy choice would have been a tandem jump, but easy was not our choice!

We had completed many hours of training and then the day finally arrived. We headed down to Fairbridge, a small locale well south of the city. No chance of city-based updraughts down there! Just some methane from all the cows and potentially some landing hazards provided by our bovine friends as well.

The plane was small. It fit the pilot and three passengers. Only two of us would be jumping from the plane. I could feel my anxiety mounting. My palms were sweaty, my mouth dry. I felt the churning in my gut and was pretty glad to have had a quick 'nervous one' in the toilet prior to take-off.

We geared up: white overalls, backpack with chute, helmet and goggles. Not an ensemble designed for any fashion event. Then we climbed into the plane and prepared for take-off. I love the feeling of small planes. So different from the jumbos we travel in for holidays. There is this indescribable feeling of weightlessness and freedom. But when you are about to jump out of one for the first time, it is hardly the thing you focus on.

I was very nervous. I was crazy nervous. I was ridiculously nervous. I was off the scale nervous. I was s%#@@ing myself to be honest.

I couldn't focus on the jump. If I did I would never have left the plane. Instead I broke it down into small chunks.

- Okay – all I need to do is ride in the plane. I can do that!
- Okay – all I need to do is move to the open door. I can do that.
- Okay – all I need to do is grab the wing strut and hang from it outside the plane. I can do that. (I think!)
- Okay – all I need to do is let go! I did that.

Once I let go and was immersed in the jump it was one of the greatest feelings of my life. The feeling of the freefall was like that tickly feeling you get in your tummy when you go over a high bump quickly in the car; but in freefalling from a plane it really lasts. Exhilarating, adrenaline charged, total excitement.

And then the static line reached its end and pulled the chute open. One thousand-two thousand-three thousand-check red. The chute was perfect. It was time to sight the arrow on the ground, keep an eye on my direction and enjoy the descent.

It was far from the big rush of freefall but I have to say it still had its charm. Absolute weightlessness, the life of a bird. The immense and amazing view. I continued the slow fall, and when I reached a certain point, out came the ping pong paddles in the hands of the instructor as he directed me to the ground. I landed perfectly.

Whoop whoops, high fives, hugs. That was tops!

NOT A TRAGEDY, THANK GOODNESS!

Tragedy: The situation or characters involved are fundamentally flawed. The flaws create continual issues and get in the way of any successful outcome. The tragedy needs to be accepted, loss mourned and the characters need to move on.

Most people would think I am referring to the loss of life from having had a failed jump. No, that is not what I mean!

This could have been a tragedy if I had allowed my fear to overwhelm me, if I had succumbed to what was threatening me and abandoned my dream of jumping out of the aeroplane. But that was not going to happen. I was too determined.

ANGELA DEFEATS THE MONSTER

Overcoming the monster: There is a conflict between us and something overwhelmingly big. We have to defeat this force that we see as monstrous and undefeatable.

There is no doubt in my mind that the final part of this parachute jump was a monster. This was an immense overcoming for me. I was petrified, afraid of heights, and was about to jump into the abyss! However, this does not encapsulate the whole experience for me. And if I had have kept the concept as a single act of overcoming the monster, I think I may have been overwhelmed by the enormity of the task and potentially failed to achieve my goal. I may have lost.

WASN'T IT A QUEST?

The quest: There is a greater goal we are seeking. We face distractions and challenges along the way to achieving this goal which contribute to the learning and growth we require; growing our capacity to achieve the bigger goal. We have help along the way and we expect this to be a lengthy commitment.

I had really approached this event as a quest and, in reality, it is structured as such by how they provided the training. We are set a series of small challenges to overcome within the training to prepare us for the jump. The instructors take the part of the wise ones who provide us with the skills and magical items (a parachute and the static line) required for our ultimate success. And

I took on the challenge with a group of sidekicks from my gym.

I broke the process down into smaller challenges that I successfully overcame, each one paving the way for the ultimate confrontation.

The team was there to support me – the group of friends from the martial arts gym who joined in (we all gave each other backing) and the boyfriend who was simply there for moral support. Together we created the group mentality of getting this thing done.

And we did. The quest served me.

In addition, as with when I had taken on the public speaking event, I had a peak experience. I experienced the rapture of having set myself a challenge that pushed the limits of my skills and gave me a sense of euphoria. Having achieved this, I grew from that and my comfort zone had shifted. I also know that if I have a team behind me and if I break a big task down into smaller parts, these aspects of the quest narrative can serve me in the future as it had in this event to achieve great things.

Such a nervous child

'This assessment will be a two-minute oral presentation,' said the teacher.

Immediately Grant's heart fluttered, his palms sweated, his mouth went dry. He had a sudden urge to pee and couldn't focus on the details of the task. Looking around, no one else seemed to be suffering. The anxiety would build inside him until the speech was done. When he stood in front of his peers, his throat would click, his palms would sweat, his voice would waver and his hands would shake.

This seemed to be a constant in his life. Grant really struggled with anxiety. It was so debilitating.

And it wasn't just oral presentations that challenged him.

Any new experience would provide him with the physical responses described above. Change of any kind was and still is challenging.

When Grant had the opportunity to change from being in an office job to going back into the classroom, he lay awake all night ruminating and stressing about the possibility. His upcoming nuptials, decades ago, were such a source of stress he was almost overcome.

And people could see it. 'You are a really nervous person,' was a common observation of his demeanour.

Fortunately for Grant and the outcome of his life, he did not allow the anxiety to overcome him. He worked hard, he tried new things and he put himself out there to grow his comfort zone.

WHAT IF HE SAW IT AS A TRAGEDY?

Tragedy: The situation or characters involved are fundamentally flawed. The flaws create continual issues and get in the way of any successful outcome. The tragedy needs to be accepted, loss mourned and the characters need to move on.

This would have been the most disastrous way of seeing the issue for Grant. I can imagine a life for him where he simply hides himself away, letting the anxiety drive him, trying to avoid anything that gave him discomfort. Slowly his world would contract until it would become unsustainable. It is fortunate for Grant that this wasn't who he chose to be despite the challenges he faces.

WAS GRANT ON A QUEST?

The quest: There is a greater goal we are seeking. We face distractions and challenges along the way to achieving this goal which contribute to the learning and growth we require; growing our capacity to achieve the bigger goal. We have help along the way and we expect this to be a lengthy commitment.

Theoretically, this could have been seen as a quest by Grant. He broke down his problem into small parts and set himself micro challenges to help him to overcome his anxiety. However, this still posited Grant's challenges as external. He could have asked for help and worked assiduously at defeating this thing every time it arose, but this was not going to result in a permanent fix for him. He needed to look within to solve this issue.

REBIRTH

Rebirth: There is a problem within ourselves that necessitates change or learning in order to resolve the conflict in our lives.

Grant did look within. He knew that he had to approach things differently if he was to cope with this issue. He put himself in situations where he felt the discomfort of nervousness and he made sure that he used positive self-talk to get himself through. Grant read every self-help book he could get his hands on. He established a set of affirmations that helped him to believe in himself. He repeated these daily. Bit by bit, Grant managed to transform himself from the nervous child to the far more confident adult. Change was still difficult for him, but he had strategies and experience so he knew that he had this thing under control. Nothing proved that more than when he and his wife decided to have children. Grant embraced this change with fervour and undertook parenthood with confidence. He became a wonderful father to his children, acting with confidence in every parenting situation, big or small. He truly had been reborn.

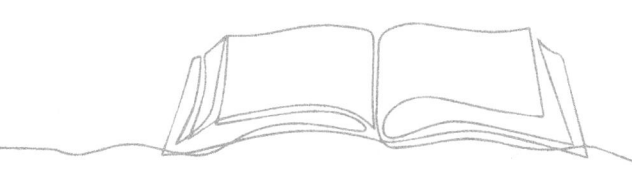

Living with grief

I never expected to attend the funeral of my super fit, 42-year-old brother. I never expected to be standing next to his way-too-young widow and three beautiful, and very young, fatherless daughters as we farewelled him from this life.

And there I was.

Nothing prepared me for the pain of grief: the cutting blade of first discovery and the enduring pain of what came after.

Nothing prepared me.

I will never forget the moment when I first found out. I was at work and hadn't checked my mobile for a while. When I did, I noticed that I had missed a whole bunch of calls and texts. I experienced that feeling when your heart beats in your throat and there is a rushing in your ears and you just know in the pit of your stomach that the news is going to be awful.

My first thought was to call my husband.

He said, 'Honey, it's the worst news.'

Well, I thought my elderly Nanna must have died. Tears sprang to my eyes expecting to hear those words, but that was not what came.

My husband did not speak further. He had lost control of his emotions, I could hear him sobbing down the phone and I shouted to him, 'You just have to tell me!'

He said, 'Michael has died.'

The world turned to hyper colour; my senses heightened. I was standing outside a building and I could see the brick wall in front of me, the very straight lines of the red brick, the cream of the mortar, the grains of sand in that mortar. I must have fallen to my knees; I could feel the roughness of the pavers on my skin. A noise seemed to rise from my stomach and through my chest, escaping my throat. I could hear it and I knew it must have been me but it seemed like it came from somewhere else. I didn't want this to be real, I didn't want it to be true and every cell in my body was screaming against this being my new reality.

And it hurt. It hurt badly.

Nothing prepared me for that excruciating first cut and nothing prepared me for the sheer longevity of the grief that followed.

My whole world changed. It's like it had shifted on its axis. Nothing was the same. I now had to process every new experience and every re-lived experience with the knowledge that my brother was no longer in this world.

Initially the pain sat with me all the time. It was all consuming and overwhelming. Getting on with the day was a near impossible task.

Over time it changed and came in waves. Those waves were big dumpers that pummelled me into the ground, blindsiding me, stealing my oxygen and taking the strength from my legs. They would come at any time. One of the major triggers was when I was going for a training run. Memories of my brother would inevitably creep in due to our shared experience in triathlon and endurance sport. The wave of grief was crippling but I needed to ride it, to see it through before I could breathe again, use my legs again, see through my tears and keep running.

And the grief endured.

I was far from my best self during this time. Instead of focusing on self-care and nurture, I would self-medicate. I would find the party people, we would drink, party, laugh and completely avoid dealing with the pain that would sit at the fringes all of the time waiting to overwhelm.

Eventually, over time, the tsunamis of grief became waves; their occurrence became less frequent. I was able to seek solace in being with people who truly cared about me and made me feel a sense of belonging and unconditional love. We started to share stories and laugh at shared experiences involving my brother. We were able to bring him up in conversation without feeling the hot knife in the chest, in fact, it seemed to help to talk about him.

And I went to a medium. This was a very healing thing for me to do. This medium was a local guy, very down to earth, and he was by no means exploitative of people like myself who had lost people close to them. He made no promises and spoke from the heart. Anthony Grzelka was able to give messages to us that promoted healing. He addressed the things that worried us most – whether Michael was in pain when he died, what he thought about the dispersal of his ashes, his appreciation of the support of certain people through the days that followed his death, his relationship with me.

Bit by bit, I have been able to adjust my way of seeing the world so that everything has its new, rightful place without him in it and having him gone is far less painful than it was.

I have come to terms with my grief.

A TRAGEDY FOR SURE

Tragedy: The situation or characters involved are fundamentally flawed. The flaws create continual issues and get in the way of any successful outcome. The tragedy needs to be accepted, loss mourned and the characters need to move on.

My forty-two-year-old brother losing his life from being hit by a car while riding his bicycle in a foreign country, widowing his young wife and leaving behind three young daughters, is absolutely a hideous tragedy. But my grief is not.

If I had accepted my grief as a tragedy, I would accept living with the level of agony of that first loss forever. I would wallow in it and not try to find reprieve. I would not seek comfort and would be trapped in the depths of despair.

GRIEF IS A MONSTER

Overcoming the monster: There is a conflict between us and something overwhelmingly big. We have to defeat this force that we see as monstrous and undefeatable.

Again, it is true that grief is a monster. But I did not have the strength or capacity to overcome the monster for a long time, so treating it as such would have been too hard. I would not have succeeded and would have been crushed under the weight of the attempt. The reality is, I actually never tried and really couldn't. And grief, in my opinion, is not a one-off battle. Although a beast, this thing is enduring.

A LONG JOURNEY

Journey and return: Our world is changed or is in some way unfamiliar, causing discomfort. We need to acquire new learning and adjust in order to succeed.

I was immersed in an unfamiliar world. I did need to learn to come to terms with my life without my brother in it. But I don't think this tells the whole story.

MY GRIEF – MY QUEST

The quest: There is a greater goal we are seeking. We face distractions and challenges along the way to achieving this goal which contribute to the learning and growth we require; growing our capacity to achieve the bigger goal. We have help along the way and we expect this to be a lengthy commitment.

There are some aspects of this experience that make the quest the most logical telling and the one that would serve me best. We know that grief is a long game. We cannot take on grief in one fell swoop and have it be gone! And it is something that is best dealt with utilising the support of others – family, friends, those who knew and loved the person who has passed. Counsellors, and if it works for you, mediums. There will be challenges along the way as the waves of grief hit, and expecting these challenges to occur constantly, then regularly then occasionally over time, is helpful in dealing with this reality. Each challenge overcome is a great assister in meeting the overarching goal of coming to terms with grief. It was certainly my quest and it is a long 'b' of an experience. Some nine years on, now, my brother's death is still one of the greatest tragedies of my life, but my grief is something that I have come to terms with and it doesn't hurt with the same ferocity it once did.

The perception of my grief as a quest is healing in and of itself. If we are clear that this thing will take time and are prepared for what is to come, dealing with the horror of grief is just a tiny bit more bearable.

Kelly covets that office

It's a really nice office. It was spacious and it was quiet. The long, white desks gleamed in their pristine state. The paint was fresh, the carpet unstained from use, the feeling was of something fresh, new and inviting.

Kelly set herself up there.

Kelly really liked having her work set up in that office. It's quiet, it's near her practical workspace. She could work in there without being disturbed or feel like anyone was looking over her shoulder. She didn't feel like everyone is watching her every move and she could just get on with things. She could spread herself out and just enjoy that lovely, open space.

Unfortunately for Kelly, this had been disallowed. She had been asked to move into a busier office space further away and her access to such things as computers and lunch making facilities within the empty office had been cut off. These things have been relocated to encourage her along.

Kelly was unhappy about this and was looking for ways to stay in her lovely office.

MONSTERS INCORPORATED

Overcoming the monster: There is a conflict between us and something overwhelmingly big. We have to defeat this force that we see as monstrous and undefeatable.

Is this workplace a giant that is exercising power over Kelly? Is she rebelliously taking on the monster? If Kelly does continue to find ways to maintain her position in the out of bounds office, she is certainly setting herself up for a stoush. She is deciding that a fight is what she wants. Will this serve her?

If Kelly goes about this in a passive aggressive manner by simply holding her space in the new office, she doesn't have the moral high ground. She is directly going against the instruction of her boss. However, if she has stated her case and her case is strong both in logic and on moral grounds, maybe this story is served by seeing it as overcoming the monster.

Kelly needs to be overtly aware, though, that in this narrative there is a winner and there is a loser. Monsters don't like to lose. Also, bosses can simply hold fast to a position and feel justified to do so. Sometimes they also see value in the suppression of rebels. It is common for power holders to react strongly when people dig their heels in. A power struggle ensues.

If Kelly tells this story as overcoming the monster, she is certainly rebelling and risks her reputation being interpreted as such. She may be poking a bear and she may lose this one. She may actually end up damaged from this fight. That would not serve her.

FUNNY BUSINESS

Comedy: There is confusion obscuring the truth. It creates problems and misunderstandings as a result.

Could this be a comedy? Is it a case of mutual misunderstanding?

All of this feels to Kelly like bullying and aggressive tactics to force her to do something against her will. She wants to be able to access an office workspace that is convenient to her practical workspace and to be able to work in peace. She feels like they just want to keep an eye on her and control her every move.

As for the 'other side', they see someone who is being rebellious. They are trying to offer an environment where she has upline support, an environment that facilitates easier channels of communication. They also need to reduce cleaning and upkeep costs while they have fewer staff in this workplace which is why they are keeping staff in fewer workspaces.

Neither group in this situation are talking to each other. They are not listening to or hearing the other side's point of view. If they did, they may be able to clear up the issues and move forward. Instead they are playing a game of chess.

However, it may be that even if they knew the situation from both sides they may be at a stale mate anyway. Hearing the other point of view doesn't mean that the person will get what they want. This may be the case here and so going for clarification might only get clarification and not a win-win outcome. The comedy, then, doesn't ultimately serve.

A TEMPORARY TRAGEDY?

Tragedy: The situation or characters involved are fundamentally flawed. The flaws create continual issues and get in the way of any successful outcome. The tragedy needs to be accepted, loss mourned and the characters need to move on.

Maybe Kelly needs to let this go for a little while. The workplace is growing and probably in one year's time there will be no choice but to open that office for occupation. Kelly will have her way. If she can let this go in the short-term, show some compliance to her employer in order to salvage her reputation and accept that it is only a matter of time before that lovely office becomes her new work home, then she may well find some peace in this situation.

Lucy learns to do a 'round-off on the beam'

Lucy can do a cartwheel on the beam. She can do a round-off on the floor. Her coach wanted her to put these skills together to master the round-off on the beam. The round-off is basically a cartwheel but the landing has two feet together and is effected after springing from the hands in an inverted position. This was the next skill that Lucy needed to master so she could get the most points possible in her level seven gymnastics competition.

She wasn't nervous. She believes that when you are nervous, it makes the skill harder to achieve. She says she avoids nervousness altogether.

In order to master this skill, it is scaffolded. First Lucy had to master it on the floor, then on a line on the floor, then on a floor beam and then finally on the beam (which is probably a metre in the air).

Lucy had mastered the skill up to the floor beam. It was time to have a go on the beam. Lucy put her two hands together on the beam and lifted herself so her weight was supported on her arms. She climbed on to the beam and then came to a standing position. She assumed a ready position, one toe pointed and the other flat. She centred herself. She took two steps beginning with the pointed toe, jumped into a 'hurdle', holding her hands in the air and one knee cocked. One foot stepped forward, and hands still raised, she moved into the side handstand commencing the cartwheel part of the trick. Her legs came together and she sprung up from her hands, intending to land with both feet together on the beam, knees bent and hands both facing forward with arms outstretched. She landed and one foot made the beam. The other did not. She fell onto the mat.

She got back up and tried again. She didn't land it. She went again. She didn't make it. She went again. She didn't make it. She went a 'million times'.

She still hasn't made it to the date of writing this. But she is still persisting. She knows she is going to make this trick. She has an unwavering belief that this can happen – if she can make it on the lower beam she can make it on the higher one. She knows to make it happen she needs to apply advice from her coach about technique, watch how others are doing it and tell herself she can. She needs to adjust her techniques as she goes. She will keep on doing this until she is successful.

IT WILL NEVER BE A TRAGEDY

Tragedy: The situation or characters involved are fundamentally flawed. The flaws create continual issues and get in the way of any successful outcome. The tragedy needs to be accepted, loss mourned and the characters need to move on.

Lucy will never give up on this trick. She is never going to say to herself, 'It's too hard,' or 'I can't do this.' She knows she can and she will not think in those terms. The minute she does start to treat this as a tragedy is the moment she has lost faith in her ability to master the skill. And she will be right – if she thinks she can't, she can't.

CINDERELLA IS NOT QUITE NAILING IT EITHER

Rags to riches: In a rags to riches narrative, we are unseen, overlooked, downtrodden and suffering. We have all the characteristics, skills and ability required to have all that we desire. But we are powerless to have these traits revealed. We have to work hard and stay true to ourselves.

Rags to riches is not quite the right approach either. Lucy is not waiting patiently for her skill to be realised. She knows that she has to keep working at this for her abilities to develop to the point where she gets this skill right every time.

REBIRTH

Rebirth: There is a problem within ourselves that necessitates change or learning in order to resolve the conflict in our lives.

This is absolutely a story of personal development. Lucy knows that she needs to keep working on herself – reflecting on what she is doing right and what she needs to tweak, and simply practice the bejeesus out of this thing to get it right. Thinking about this as a rebirth, knowing that she needs to do the work to get this thing done, is the most empowering narrative Lucy can apply in this situation. Once she has got all of the changes together in herself, she WILL nail this skill.

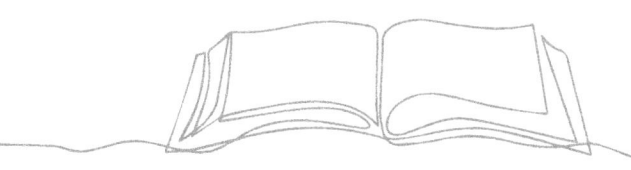

A personal mission

Plastic has always bothered me. Did you know that every piece of plastic ever made on this earth still exists? And after watching that hard-hitting short documentary on YouTube about Midway Island and seeing in Al Gore's *An Inconvenient Truth* (2006) imagery of the Pacific Garbage Dump, I have been on a bit of a personal crusade to try to reduce the single use plastic in my life and avoid being a contributor to this disaster.

But plastic is EVERYWHERE.

The first thing I did was to stop using plastic wrap for food. This was initially challenging as I had to find alternatives. I started putting things in the fridge in a bowl with a plate on top. This was not quite airtight enough to provide the longevity in the food that I desired when storing it in the fridge. I have experimented with reusable silicone covers. These were okay, but not particularly reliable. I have decided that the best thing to do is have a set of robust, reusable plastic containers that I look after well so that they last a lifetime. I now store all foods that require wrapping in these. Probably the hardest issue to overcome was wrapping sandwiches for kids' lunches. That was a bit of a journey. First, I went to baking paper but discovered it has content that is not environmentally friendly, thus is not much better than plastic wrap, if at all. We tried brown paper. This did not keep the sandwiches fresh. Beeswax wraps are nice but they seem to suffer when the temperature is warm, as it often is when our kids' bags are outside during the school day. I finally settled on sandwich-sized boxes that could keep the sandwich together and keep the food fresh but also fit into the category of highly reusable. I want these containers to be used for at least the rest of my life, if not longer. And if I no longer have a use for them, I am a firm believer in handing things on so their use continues.

I was a big user of plastic shopping bags. I justified this because I used the bags as rubbish bin liners. I had no ideas for an alternative to this. It was a choice of either using my shopping bags or buying plastic liners. I found a rubbish bag alternative made from plant-based products that are supposed to be fully biodegradable. No more excuses! I have since invested in more reusable shopping bags than any person truly needs. I actually make the reusable shopping bag my souvenir when I travel. I love my Coober Pedy IGA bag and my Yosemite convenience store bag equally! This was a pretty easy transition, only held back by trying to engender the habit of grabbing the bags when I leave the car. And now that we have laws about single use plastic bags in Australia, everyone has BYO shopping bags or has to buy a set when they shop. A fabulous movement forward for the planet.

Our fruit and vegetables are still able to be bagged in plastic, though. I never take those flimsy, single use bags. I grab my fruit and veg and pile them into the trolley and onto the checkout, then into my reusable bag without pre-bagging them. This is quite entertaining when I buy snow peas. I have bought small string bags to use for this purpose but have never managed to add using them into my regular behaviours. That's okay, what I do seems to work. However, there are still some things that remain a bit tricky. That includes products that maintain their freshness in plastic, like washed salad leaves. Without plastic packaging they wilt and are hard, if not impossible to sell to people. But there must be a way of dealing with this. My friend, Jamo, has introduced me to a way of storing whole lettuce so that this is a non-issue. Wrapping the lettuce in the outer leaves keeps the inner leaves fresh for long enough to consume the bits of the lettuce that we choose to eat. Some fruits like cherries and grapes are only sold in single use bags too. I may have to look at my choices with those products, using some consumer power to help effect change. Bread is difficult. It is sold in plastic bags because that keeps the bread fresh and the slices together. It is also convenient to freeze in these bags. I suppose that if I took the loaf home whole, I could slice and package it at home but those machines do such a good job of slicing! And, then, what do I put it in? I haven't yet figured out a way of packaging bread that serves. I reconcile myself by reusing the bags the bread comes in. The bag gets shaken out when the bread is done and stored for later use. It will often be reused many times, the process of reusing includes the bag being washed if necessary.

I have trained my family to avoid plastic wrap and single use plastic bags. Their fervour is not necessarily as strong as mine, but each of us are doing our own little bit. And the kids will take these better habits out into the world with them. Hopefully, if we can all do something like this we can save our suffocating planet.

We need to, it's the only one we've got.

PLEASE DON'T SEE OUR PLANET AS A TRAGEDY!

Tragedy: The situation or characters involved are fundamentally flawed. The flaws create continual issues and get in the way of any successful outcome. The tragedy needs to be accepted, loss mourned and the characters need to move on.

> What's the point in doing anything? The planet is buggered anyway. I am only one person amongst billions. Have you seen the plastic that washes up on Kuta Beach every day? Bulldozers come and clear it away. Daily. I can't do anything to change that. How can I possibly make a difference? There is no point.

If we all looked at what we have done to the planet as a tragedy, none of us would do anything to reverse the damage we are causing. We would simply give up, suggesting, as the words above say, that our individual contribution will have no effect. We would choose to not do anything because we would see our planet as done-for. However, let's consider what China did to clear the air in Beijing for the Olympic games and how being in lock down in our major cities because of COVID-19 has had a massive, positive impact on the air quality in our major cities across the globe. These results suggest we can yet make a difference.

I certainly don't want to write off our planet and urge everyone else not to consider this story a tragedy either.

THIS WHOLE THING IS A MONSTER

Overcoming the monster: There is a conflict between us and something overwhelmingly big. We have to defeat this force that we see as monstrous and undefeatable.

We cannot deny the size of the issue of environmental degradation, disaster and climate change. However, if we employ the concept of this being a monster, how on Earth will we ever, as individuals, find the wherewithal – the tools, the capacity, the very energy – to defeat this thing. It simply does not serve me, or any other individual on the planet, to construct environmental issues as a monster to overcome because we are so small in comparison. We do not have the tools to defeat it alone. We will not see ourselves as able and will probably not even try. We don't want to be the losers in this thing, or for our planet to lose either.

A REBIRTH?

Rebirth: There is a problem within ourselves that necessitates change or learning in order to resolve the conflict in our lives.

I could consider myself changed to a person who no longer uses single use plastics as I have previously done. I have made that change in my life, transformed myself as such. However, this is not a single dimensional story. I have not learnt one thing and made one change. The rebirth doesn't quite fit for me. I feel like there is more to it.

A LEARNING JOURNEY

Journey and return: Our world is changed or is in some way unfamiliar, causing discomfort. We need to acquire new learning and adjust in order to succeed.

I feel that I am on a pathway of improvement. I keep picking up little tips and tricks, as well as reshaping my thoughts and beliefs along the way with regard to dealing with this issue of plastics in my world. As I travel down the highway of this new world of environmentalism, becoming more environmentally aware, I become more knowledgeable about behaving in ways that reduce plastics and then can apply this to my life. And there is always new inspiration, new inventions, improved initiatives and better government policies that assist in helping me to behave in more environmentally friendly ways. In fact, the interest in plastic reduction then becomes one part of a more environmentally aware attitude which then impacts my life broadly. I start looking at other ways to implement change – taking the car out less, eating fewer animal products, putting solar panels on the roof. Being willing to learn and grow in this environmentally aware world assists in being able to be proactive about the environment. This narrative serves me in keeping positive, keeping open minded and doing my small bit to save the planet.

I am now three years without having used a single piece of plastic wrap!

I hope you are on this journey with me.

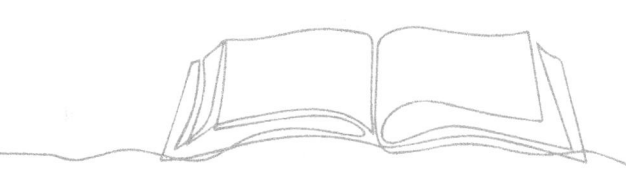

Redecorating the house

John looked around his house for the umpteenth time and said to himself, 'I really need to do something about this. This place is a dump.'

To be honest, John is a bit of a hermit. He works from home and he hardly goes out. His house can sometimes feel like a prison with the walls closing in on him. And the walls were dirty. They were chipped. And they were a tragic shade of yellowy cream. He really didn't know what he was thinking when he painted the walls that colour ten years ago.

The more he looked at the house, the more work he saw. Not only were the walls dirty but the door frames were in need of a painting as well. And the ceiling, does that need a lick of paint? What colour to choose? Should he paint all of the walls the same colour? What do the experts say? Does he really need to choose a warm white for the bedrooms and a cool white for the lounge?

Finally, he was on holidays and he decided it was time. He commenced work.

As he started to prep the walls, the job grew. He discovered that the original painters hadn't sealed the walls and the paint that was on the walls came off in large strips when he removed the light switches. He worked out that he would need to peel the paint from all of the walls before he sealed it and painted again. He peeled paint for days and filled his wheelie bin with the detritus. He found that the skirting boards were in the way so, cursing, he resolved to remove them for the task. He wasn't happy with the placement of the picture hooks so he removed them also and filled and sanded the holes. Shelves in the cupboard? Too hard to paint around, let's move them out.

The door frames had large chips and would need to be sanded back before painting. The doors were in the way and would need to be removed before he could sand effectively. The noise of the sander was horrific and put him into a foul mood.

This job was bigger than Ben Hur. John had two weeks' holiday. His house was in disarray. He got one room painted. His worst nightmare BUT he was committed to the task and still planned to get this all done. Now he just had to fit it around work.

A POTENTIAL TRAGEDY

Tragedy: The situation or characters involved are fundamentally flawed. The flaws create continual issues and get in the way of any successful outcome. The tragedy needs to be accepted, loss mourned and the characters need to move on.

If John had built this job in his mind to the point where it was too big to achieve, he would have written it off and never commenced the task. The state of his house would have been a tragedy never to be resolved. However, it would always have disturbed him, grown to becoming a bane and he would have been trapped in the nightmare of this narrative as a tragedy, not being able to get past it. This narrative would not serve him.

JOHN HAS MADE A MONSTER

Overcoming the monster: There is a conflict between us and something overwhelmingly big. We have to defeat this force that we see as monstrous and undefeatable.

John never actually wanted to do the work required to get this job done. He always saw it as something that was distasteful but was necessary. He despised the house and the way it looked. It was hideous.

And his thought patterns had him growing the task into some kind of monstrous beast that needed to be overcome, a mountain, a mammoth. And he needed to do it himself.

Does this serve John?

John had the skills and capacity to get the job done. He had allocated time to it. He was committed to the task. All of these things meant that he could be served by the narrative of overcoming the monster. However, in approaching his renovations in this narrative he was attempting to eat the elephant in one gulp, and to continue the metaphor, he couldn't get his mouth around it! He had set up the house to complete the rennos in one hit. He spent a lot of time in preparation for this and in doing so, his house was a complete mess. And then time ran out. He never felt any further from completion. This was a source of mounting frustration for John as he peered around his unkempt home.

Was overcoming the monster the narrative that served him? Is there a narrative that would help him have a more positive mindset?

A DECORATIVE QUEST?

The quest: There is a greater goal we are seeking. We face distractions and challenges along the way to achieving this goal which contribute to the learning and growth we require; growing our capacity to achieve the bigger goal. We have help along the way and we expect this to be a lengthy commitment.

If John broke the job down into smaller challenges, like filling the holes, sanding the frames, completing one room at a time and so on, and rewarded himself (with praise, self-satisfaction or a bourbon even!) for each accomplishment, he may find the task more palatable. He could seek help from some kind-hearted friends (sidekicks) to hasten the completion of the task and reduce his workload. In fact, he did invite all who utilised his toilet to peel some paint while they were in there. Now the euphemism exists in his house: should one need to use the toilet they are going to 'peel some paint'. And some magical tools could come in handy: rollers, spray guns, edging tools, supplied by friends or the ever-helpful people down at Bunnings. And while at the hardware giant, sustenance is available in the form of a sausage sizzle. What a box ticker!

Seeing this as a quest, a long journey expectedly full of arduous and challenging tasks that he is willing to take on but broken into small challenges with rewards and respite at set junctures, would set John up with the mindset required to take on the work of redecorating that he set himself. This would keep him positive and goal focused while enduring the challenges of the tasks along the way. The narrative seen as a quest has John understanding from the outset that this is a long game and has him expecting challenges and small achievements on his journey toward home improvement.

The quest would serve John.

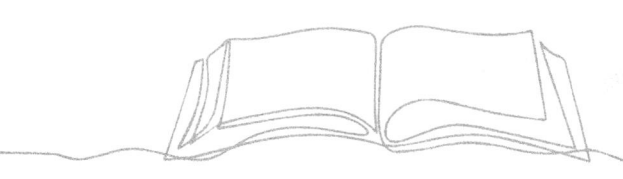

A bully for a boss

A while ago Marie was in a job that was not going well.

Her work situation was untenable. Her boss was a bully and she had it in for Marie. The boss looked for opportunities to call Marie on substandard performance and 'what we look for we find'. Marie's performance was far from below par, but when someone is so convinced that their lens is accurate, this is difficult to shift. Often, the boss attributed others' work to Marie when it was not hitting the mark. If something had a whiff of Marie's involvement, her boss would deliberately put a halt to it. She would arbitrarily create bureaucratic processes to put blockers in the way of things that were in Marie's realm of work or sphere of influence. She removed Marie's access to data sources that would allow her to strategically plan. She disallowed volunteer support for a project Marie had proposed. She misinterpreted policy and used it in public ways to denounce Marie's actions around some tasks. She would say that Marie had done and said things that she had had no part in.

She really had it in for Marie.

Marie felt like she couldn't do her job effectively. She felt like her reputation was being trashed by this woman and she was powerless to do anything about it. The boss was making her question herself when she spoke so certainly about Marie's alleged conversations and actions that had actually not taken place. Marie was immensely frustrated by the injustice she was feeling. Her health was suffering, mentally and physically.

WAS SHE A MONSTER?

Overcoming the monster: There is a conflict between us and something overwhelmingly big. We have to defeat this force that we see as monstrous and undefeatable.

It was very easy for Marie to fall into creating the internal narrative of the boss as a monster. However, this filled the boss with power and took it away from Marie. She was effectively feeding the power the boss had over her by imagining her as the monster. Because of her role as the boss and the way she was behaving, Marie had no control over what was happening and her boss had immense capacity to cause harm to Marie. She could not see any way to overcome this. Any plans to defend herself would just look like she couldn't see the truth of her own failings. She was really disempowered by perceiving the story in this way. Any potential tools Marie could fathom were no match for the monster. And if they went head to head, Marie probably would have lost. Marie could not get out of the nightmare stage of this narrative.

IS THIS JUST A BIG MIX UP?

Comedy: There is confusion obscuring the truth. It creates problems and misunderstandings as a result.

In some ways the comedy might have served Marie. If Marie was willing to just keep plugging away at her work, making sure others could see what was really going on, eventually the truth of the situation may have been revealed. Marie would be seen as the capable professional she had always been perceived as elsewhere and the boss would be revealed as the confused and crazy one. This may have given Marie a level of acceptance of the situation without infusing anyone with any power over her. She could simply shake her head at what she saw as her boss' failings. This had its shortcomings, though. She might either behave passively, hoping that people would see her truth, or she could work actively to discredit her boss and push people along to her own version of what was true. If Marie chose to try to convince others of the 'reality' of the situation, she risked them not seeing things from her point of view. This could have massive detrimental effects on how she was perceived as a professional and have Marie acting in shadow trying to clear the confusion at play. A tricky state of affairs that made Marie feel uncomfortable even as she contemplated it, showing a lack of integrity: she would need to badmouth her boss, which didn't feel great to her whether the negative comments were true or false. Not healthy. Not productive. She didn't think there was anything to be gained.

A TRAGEDY?

Tragedy: The situation or characters involved are fundamentally flawed. The flaws create continual issues and get in the way of any successful outcome. The tragedy needs to be accepted, loss mourned and the characters need to move on.

This certainly could have been posed as a tragedy. The great hope for the 'best job ever'. A boss who Marie thought was the ants' pants until... A chance to really make her mark and achieve great things within an area that was new to Marie and had great potential for a person in her position to find success. A good job that would perhaps offer a pathway to promotion. And then it all went wrong. Turned out the boss wasn't who Marie thought she was. All of these dreams and plans were dashed. Marie could keep turning this over in her head and keep in the nightmare stage of this tragedy, even though it was long ago. Or she could get to some level of acceptance and simply put it to bed as a tragedy and a loss. Unfortunately, this was not working for Marie. In telling the narrative this way, Marie felt her stomach full of unresolved emotions. She was ruminating. She was still stuck. This narrative was doing Marie a disservice. There must be a narrative that serves Marie better.

A JOURNEY FOR MARIE, PERHAPS?

Journey and return: Our world is changed or is in some way unfamiliar, causing discomfort. We need to acquire new learning and adjust in order to succeed.

This could well have been considered a journey and return. Marie was most definitely thrust into an unfamiliar world; it was not the one she had signed up for. Things had changed immensely from when she started the role. Could she have put the experiences down to learning opportunities and reflect on how she emerged from this experience the wiser for all of this which had occurred? This certainly has potential for Marie to be accepting of the circumstances and willing to take on all events and ill treatment as something that ultimately has helped her to grow. She would need to be careful not to repeat this pattern of accepting being treated poorly because she has this story posited as a learning opportunity. No matter what she can learn from being bullied, no one deserves that kind of treatment and if it occurred again, she needed to be prepared to take action.

Perhaps there is another slant on this, and Marie was simply adjusting to new ways of communicating and a different power regime. If she could have learned to communicate within this new paradigm and accept the way the power structure worked, perhaps Marie could have fit into this new world instead of expecting it to fit her? If she thought this way, there is a feeling of the tragedy narrative creeping in because her chance to do anything about this has gone. However, if she could keep focused on the learning, she could focus on the fact that she can now see this perspective from the outside because of the experience. Marie could keep thinking that she now may be more able to be that self-aware in future positions. Because of all of this journey and return narrative style thinking, she could keep positively framed and have this narrative serve her.

A MOMENT OF REFLECTION

Although this was a situation from her distant past, it is interesting the impact it has had on Marie to relive the story which felt so traumatising to her at the time. Initially she became immersed in the emotions again, the injustice of it really played on her. However, in processing the event by applying the different narratives, she had this sense of control over things where, as the victim, she did not. She felt a release in her body as she spoke about this being a journey and return; the challenges she faced being opportunities for Marie to grow in order to be able to deal with that new world and be better equipped when her world changed again. Also, in considering it a learning opportunity, she felt the power with which she had imbued that boss ebbing away. She felt a desire to take on more challenges; felt stronger and like this is all in her interests as she worked toward reframing the narrative and feeling healthier about what was a tricky time in her life. It felt to her like going through the process of reframing what happened in the past to a narrative that served her had actually helped her to overcome that past trauma.

A beastly husband

'Where have you been?' the voice is angry, infused with aggression.

'Out to the shops, Hun.'

'Where have you been?' The voice becomes more aggressive and demanding. 'You have been gone for hours.'

'I have been gone for just over an hour. Here's the shopping.' She tries to keep her body language open and her voice meek, hoping he leaves it at that. She does *not* want to 'poke the bear'. They had been going so well, it had been ages since he last lost it, but she could feel it brewing. He always worked himself up to it.

'You are taking the mick. How much money did you spend?' the jibes continue.

'About a hundred bucks, Hun.' Endearments to soften him. He doesn't respond to this gesture. He thunders toward her, tearing into the shopping bags looking for something to prove his suspicions of her failings.

'Where is the coke?' he demands, looming over her. That kernel of fear took root in her stomach. 'Where's the fucking coke?' This voice is quieter but infinitely more menacing, hissed through clenched teeth and she is sure his fists are the same. 'You are useless,' he shouts and pushes her backwards from him. She falls and strikes her side on the door frame. She lays crumpled on the floor, in pain and trying to catch her breath.

'It's okay, Hun, I will go back for it. It will only take me a minute.'

POOR CINDERELLA

Rags to riches: In a rags to riches narrative, we are unseen, overlooked, downtrodden and suffering. We have all the characteristics, skills and ability required to have all that we desire. But we are powerless to have these traits revealed. We have to work hard and stay true to ourselves.

Julie was a dutiful wife living with an abusive husband. She stayed in the marriage for twenty-four years. She never stopped trying to please him and he never stopped finding ways to control her and abuse her.

But Julie stood by him.

She was the housekeeper; he would never dream of lifting a finger inside the house. If he was on holidays and she was working, she would have to do these duties when she got home. He didn't like her going out, would harass her leading up to it and question her mercilessly afterward to try to catch her out in some wrongdoing. He would stalk her to make sure she was where she said she would be.

She was subject to his violent rages, at times she thought he was going to kill her.

But she remained faithful and dutiful and looked after him in every way she could, hoping against hope that he would recognise these qualities in her and it would bring out the prince in him.

Needless to say that this narrative was doing Julie a real disservice. She was simply stuck in this tyrannous marriage. She needed to escape the oppression of her abusive husband and lay that marriage to rest.

IT TRULY WAS A TRAGEDY

Tragedy: The situation or characters involved are fundamentally flawed. The flaws create continual issues and get in the way of any successful outcome. The tragedy needs to be accepted, loss mourned and the characters need to move on.

There was nothing that Julie had been able to do to change the reality of this marriage in all of those years of dutiful service. Julie was far better served when she came to see the marriage in terms of a tragedy – something that was lost and over. Her husband was a fatally flawed character in the story, unable to be rebirthed or redeemed. Once having made that realisation, this set Julie on a path of action. Her narrative changed again.

AN ESCAPE QUEST

The quest: There is a greater goal we are seeking. We face distractions and challenges along the way to achieving this goal which contribute to the learning and growth we require; growing our capacity to achieve the bigger goal. We have help along the way and we expect this to be a lengthy commitment.

Julie's ultimate prize was to escape from the marriage. She knew this would take some long-term planning and that she would need to time it right. She had a series of attempts that did not work out. A couple of times she went to shelters but he managed to weasel her back when she was returning to cook and clean for her boys who did not want to go to the shelter with her. Eventually *he* decided the marriage was over and Julie was able to effect her escape. The story narrated to herself as a quest kept Julie focused on her end game with her eyes on the prize. She persisted even when she experienced failures and setbacks, and she eventually triumphed.

Julie's narrative changed over time. However, it only began to serve her once she had determined that the relationship was a lost cause. The quest gave her the chance to break her escape down into small parts, to embrace the failed attempts as part of the overall journey toward emancipation. To see the breakup of the marriage as something to achieve over a period of time rather than in an instance.

The quest served her.

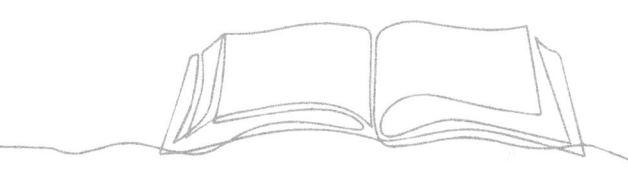

Sally is the scapegoat

Sally had been in an unsustainable work situation. 2020 may have brought COVID-19, but along with it came a whole host of neuroses that we could never have imagined. And these seemed to play out in Sally's workplace. She became ensnared amongst the interplay of such craziness.

The people at an executive level in her workplace had determined that things were not functioning well in Sally's department. Sally was in a low-level leadership position, had very little power and simply wanted to keep doing her job. Her reputation until now was sterling. She was well respected in her field, was intelligent and certainly knew her stuff. People would come to her for advice and support so she was a natural choice for a promotional position.

However, in this workplace there were a lot of new 'players'. People were trying to find their place in the pecking order and to develop their ways of communicating with each other; in the greater hierarchy this was also taking place. This was all against the backdrop of a pretty high pressure, high stress environment where people could get hurt if poor decisions were made or actions were not in keeping with best practice as well as policy and procedure. A lot of times, the people in the middle of the hierarchy were inexperienced or under trained. Quite often those perceived as lower on the totem pole were best placed to provide the right advice and information required for everyone to be safe.

Unfortunately, in this work place, a lot of egos were at play. Some of the players in the hierarchy were not prepared to have those in lower hierarchical positions provide them with advice. Those at the top of the totem pole also felt the same, inferring that it was better that people get hurt than people step outside of the hierarchy. With this as the overarching attitude, suppression (oppression?) of those at the lower end of the totem pole was inevitable.

With tender egos and inexperience in the middle of the hierarchy and some pretty experienced people at the lower end of the hierarchy, tension arose. The executive level leaders tried to get to the bottom of what was going on but were quick to jump to conclusions. They incorrectly determined that Sally was ground zero for the issues that were occurring within her department.

They brought Sally in to the boss' office and gave her a talking to. They believed she was providing advice outside her station. They gave her a very strong 'cease and desist' message. Sally was confused. She could not understand what she had done to get things so wrong. She felt like her legs had been cut out from under her and her tongue from her mouth. She no longer could do her job, nor could she speak up against the injustice she faced. She also knew that they had misunderstood the work environment and without the growth and change required of those working there, people WOULD get hurt. She was beside herself. She could not see a path forward.

Sally's initial reaction to this event was extreme. Sally went into shut down. She could no longer attend work, she spent hours curled up in a ball, crying her eyes out. She was a shell. However, her experience throughout this was interesting. Her way of narrating the story to herself over time evolved, but it really needed to.

SALLY IS PITTED AGAINST THE MONSTER

Overcoming the monster: There is a conflict between us and something overwhelmingly big. We have to defeat this force that we see as monstrous and undefeatable.

This is crazy. They have no idea what is actually going on here and they are blaming me for everything that is going wrong. Who are these people? They are making assumptions that are so far off base that it's ridiculous and yet here we are at the 'coal face' having to work in pretty extreme conditions, when they are not putting in the training required and people are getting hurt. I don't want to get hurt and I don't want anyone else getting hurt.

But they won't listen. I have no voice. They won't hear what I have got to say. They have made a situation where I cannot work. It's not fair. It's too hard. I can't face it any more.

Sally was clearly feeling that she was pitted against a monster that was undefeatable. She felt so disempowered by this work situation that she could no longer even face the monster. This had taken away her strength to the point where she was a total mess. This was a real David and Goliath situation. She was pitted against a giant, yet, unlike David, did not feel that she was equipped for this battle. Telling her story in this way led her well on the path to an emotional breakdown.

A NEAR TRAGEDY

Tragedy: The situation or characters involved are fundamentally flawed. The flaws create continual issues and get in the way of any successful outcome. The tragedy needs to be accepted, loss mourned and the characters need to move on.

I can't do this. I am going to quit.

Feeling like she could not overcome this situation very nearly led to a tragedy. This exceptionally capable and talented worker was set to quit her job and withdraw her service because she felt unable to work under the conditions she faced. However, if Sally left under these conditions, she would be eternally trapped in the nightmare stage of the tragedy and would not be able to find peace.

SALLY ENLISTS HELP IN HER QUEST

The quest: There is a greater goal we are seeking. We face distractions and challenges along the way to achieving this goal which contribute to the learning and growth we require; growing our capacity to achieve the bigger goal. We have help along the way and we expect this to be a lengthy commitment.

> *I can't take this on by myself. I need help. I don't want to be dealing with this by myself. I don't want to be suffering like this either.*

Sally had known mental health issues from a third party perspective for a long time. It just took her a while to recognise where she was at as a result of her experiences. After a while she started to look at her reaction to the situation from the outside and saw her behaviour as a mental health issue and knew she needed help to get through. Once Sally shifted the story she was telling herself from being overwhelmed and 'I can't' to seeing herself as needing help, her situation started to change. In this instance, she has changed the narrative to a quest. The quest allowed her to enlist support from a team of people who could help her overcome her obstacles and reach a satisfactory outcome. The ultimate goal was still a long way off and she knew she had significant work to put in before she got there but she had help. She sought support from a psychologist. This professional helped her to break down her recovery into manageable chunks or smaller challenges. With these new skills and with a series of successes, she was able to rebuild herself and slowly found herself able to face her situation and return to work.

SALLY SEES HERSELF ON A LEARNING JOURNEY

Journey and return: Our world is changed or is in some way unfamiliar, causing discomfort. We need to acquire new learning and adjust in order to succeed.

> *I need to stick it out here. I still have things to learn and this difficult situation has things to teach me.*

As Sally put a lot of the deep emotions from this experience behind her and found herself feeling stronger, her narration changed again. She knew that this workplace was not ideal – in some ways it was even toxic – but she felt that it had been educational. She had taken the power to harm out of the situation and turned it into a potential positive. This was highly empowering for Sally. She no longer infused others with the power to hurt her, in fact, she turned any potential situation where they behaved in abusive or inappropriate ways into opportunities for her to grow as a person. She had the power and this narrative truly served her. However, Sally had to be careful not to excuse poor behaviour or immerse herself unendingly in a toxic environment, convincing herself it was good for her. She may run the risk of putting up with things that she shouldn't if she maintained this narrative. There may come a point where she would need to see the whole thing as a tragedy and leave the workplace behind her, finding an environment that honoured her skill, ability and personality. But she will come to this realisation at the right time, if she needs to, and will have done the work to have found closure to the narrative so she will not be trapped in the nightmare stage of the tragedy narrative.

By reflecting throughout her experience and changing her narrative over time, Sally was able to see herself through a very difficult time in her professional life. She was able to steer her way through turbulent waters and navigate for herself the best way forward. Sally regained control of her life.

A century of problems in the family

Margaret is diminutive. That encapsulates it, really. She is a tiny slip of a person, barely reaching 4 foot 11. She has walked this earth nearly one hundred years and her crinkled face is testimony to the years of laughter, love and deep concern that have characterised her life.

Margaret is a deep thinker and has always pursued matters of intellect. She has a profound concern for the environment and feels keenly the scars we make on this world and particularly those that impact her local environment.

Mostly, Margaret has a deep care for her family. Her children are now old enough to be considered elderly themselves (but don't pass that message on to them please!).

However, there are problems within this family. Yawning, pervasive problems, seemingly unresolvable and heart breaking problems.

Margaret cannot seem to keep her relationship with her son on an even keel. They will go through periods of calm but then flare ups will occur. Margaret will, in her communication with her son, offer some age-old 'wisdom' which will cause immense offense to her son and spark a row.

The latest was in an email. Margaret was commiserating with her son on the perils of the first Christmas without a loved one who had recently passed. She provided him with some advice to help him to overcome his grief.

Unfortunately for her son, he was mired in his grief and not open to advice. Neither did he appreciate the particular advice that was given. From the outside, it certainly could be conceived as tactless. From Jimmy's point of view, it was devastating and it was not the first time. Jimmy feels this latest action was unforgivable. He communicated as much to his sibling.

GRAHAM HAS TO OVERCOME THE MONSTER

Overcoming the monster: There is a conflict between us and something overwhelmingly big. We have to defeat this force that we see as monstrous and undefeatable.

> *Mum has done it again. I can't believe that she keeps doing this. She needs to be stopped. She can't keep hurting Jimmy this way. She needs to learn her lesson and she needs to stop.*

Graham is the elder sibling and has always been Jimmy's saviour. In keeping with his role, he has established the overcoming the monster narrative for this life event. He has cast Margaret as the monster, a powerful being who can cause immense harm. He has pitted himself against her, involving himself in this family argument as the hero ready to slay the beast. He gathers his best arguments, ready to move in for the stoush. He wants to win.

This image in itself is absurd – a tiny nonagenarian who requires a walker to move around her nursing home is infused with enormous power to cause harm. A sixty-something, powerfully built man has determined himself to be the 'slayer of the monster'.

Beyond absurd, though, is that this thinking is also incredibly disempowering. Think Hercules fighting the Hydra. Every head that is chopped off this monster results in two heads growing in its place. This is the history of this family conflict. Graham will attempt to change his mother's behaviour, he will even enlist help, but she does not change. Her behaviours are consistent. Graham would need to have the strength and ingenuity of a mythical figure to be able to effect the change he desires – to defeat this 'monster'.

After a while, Graham's anger fades and his need for urgent action recedes. He begins to change his narrative.

GRAHAM SEES THE ABSURDITY

Comedy: There is confusion obscuring the truth. It creates problems and misunderstandings as a result.

> *I just don't understand how they can't get this right. If they could just see things from each other's point of view. I know Mum loves Jimmy. She loves him so much. But she just can't seem to stop saying things or writing things that really upset Jim. And Jimmy is so sensitive; I don't understand why he can't just*

let these things go. If he was just less prickly about everything then they would get on so much better. Mum says things and she does things but we don't have to let them get to us. If they could just understand each other everything would be fine!

In this way of thinking, Graham is narrating this life experience as a classic comedy. He sees confusion in their communication and hidden truths that if they could just be revealed, the two would have a workable, loving relationship. By narrating the story this way, Graham actually feels some responsibility for helping them overcome the barriers between them and to reveal their true selves to each other, so they can find happiness in themselves and their relationship. However, Graham has spent decades trying to help these two understand each other. To keep narrating the story as a comedy would only serve if there was truly a chance that the characters in the narrative could come to some kind of understanding of each other.

Maybe it is time to let go.

GRAHAM LAMENTS THE TRAGEDY

Tragedy: The situation or characters involved are fundamentally flawed. The flaws create continual issues and get in the way of any successful outcome. The tragedy needs to be accepted, loss mourned and the characters need to move on.

Oh, dear, Mum has done it again. She has gone and upset Jimmy. Another day, another email or text! Jimmy is really upset. I wonder if they will speak again after this one. Mum is never going to change. I have certainly tried to educate her in the past to write in ways that are newsy and light but she always defaults to these snippets of advice that are poorly expressed. And, of course, Jimmy takes offence. A lifetime of Mum writing advice and Jimmy taking offence. This is never going to change. It is a real shame for them but I can't see their relationship ever being anything different. Mum is 96 now, she will never change. And Jimmy is so damaged from his repeated traumatic experiences, he simply doesn't have the resilience to cope with Mum's ways.

In this new iteration of the story, Graham has transitioned to structuring this experience as a tragedy. This would be one of those times in our lives where perceiving something as a tragedy is actually the most productive course of action. Seeing that there really is nothing anyone else can do about this situation; understanding that the characters involved are fatally flawed and their relationship is destined to exist in this devolving mode. Stepping back from feeling that he has to do something about it – to fix it – when in nearly fifty years there has been no evidence this is possible, means that he can show the appropriate sympathies to the poor people involved but not invest his energy into trying to solve the unsolvable. He could put some energy into mourning the relationship and move on.

The narrative of the tragedy serves him.

It may well serve the others in similar situations, allowing them to see that nothing is going to change and acceptance is the only way forward.

PART 4

The Seven Stories We Tell Ourselves toolbox

Using the toolbox: learning to 'live consciously'

Previous sections of this book have illustrated the seven narratives and provided evidence for how they can appear in our life stories. The accounts show how we can adjust our telling of the stories of our lives, past, present and future, to ensure we are feeling in control of the events of our lives. We can choose the pathway forward or reflections of the past that truly serve us. We can narrate the events in our present state in ways that allow us acceptance and agency.

In this section you will find a host of strategies and approaches surrounding the seven stories. These are intended to allow you to use the knowledge you have gained about the seven narratives we have available, as illustrated in the previous chapters, and apply them to guide your perceptions of your own existence. Some of the strategies are intended to put you in a headspace where you can allow yourself to do this.

The toolbox is there to provide a framework and strategies to assist in applying the learning. This section holds information that allows you to be able to recognise the stories you are telling yourself. Once you become familiar with the framework, you will be able to identify any patterns that exist in your narrations.

The tools help you to go through the self-examination process and determine which of the narratives will serve you. There are some guides about how each narrative may generally do this so that you may be able to recognise this for yourself according to your own unique circumstances. You should also be able to visualise how your life would be if you were to adopt a different telling of your story. You can then apply tools to rescript your life so that you readily adopt the new narrative or apply your current narrative in more productive ways.

This toolbox also asks you to really understand your values and conduct yourself according to your values, so you genuinely believe you deserve to have a positive outcome in your story.

You will need to approach your life reflectively and with a growth mindset if you are expecting the *Seven Stories* to work for you. You may also need to be aware of and prepared to deal with your emotional states. You will need to observe your feelings and recognise when they are getting in the way, then apply strategies to change how you are feeling so you can be in a position to be objective about your life experiences and ready to reframe.

The ultimate aim is that you are empowered to make deliberate decisions about the unfolding of your life. You can narrate your stories in such a way that you are able to deal with the circumstances before you. When the issues are laid out, you can also have a clear idea of the pathway ahead as you seek resolution to the concerns in your life.

When you have mastered the application of the tools, you will be well placed to be able to take control of your thoughts. You will have the skills and strategies to cope with what life throws at you and to be able to see a pathway forward.

You will be able to live consciously.

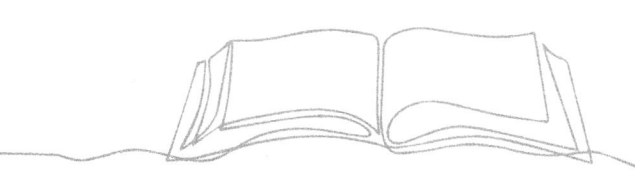

The power of a growth mindset

The ways in which we tell our stories, unless we are reflective and deliberate about it, are basically habitual. If we are behaving according to habit, then we are not making deliberate choices about our lives. We are allowing habits to drive our destiny.

This is not living our best life. This is not *living consciously*.

We need to get away from habit-based thinking and acting. We need to be mindful in our lives; be prepared to recognise and change our habits. However, in order to change our habits, we need to believe in our ability to change. We need to have a positive mindset about it.

You do need the capacity to believe that things will get better - **Charles Duhigg**

The belief that we can change could be seen as having a *growth mindset*. Its opposite is a *fixed mindset*.

If I have a fixed mindset, I will be trapped in the idea that there is no point in trying something or doing things differently because things will always turn out the same way. A classic for this is in education and learning. I actually believe I am not good at Maths. I find numbers mysterious and unfathomable most of the time. I know that if I count a group of kids, I will get a different amount every time, so I don't try. I always get someone else to do that job. Just like me with my Maths, people with a fixed mindset believe that our characteristics and abilities are innate and unchangeable.

Contrary to this is a growth mindset – we believe that we can grow and improve; that our abilities and characteristics can be changed over time. We can be better than what we are today. If I approached my mathematical ability with a growth mindset, I would be convinced that I could improve my counting skill. I would keep trying and I would apply strategies that would support more effective counting. I may even seek advice and training to help. The fact is that if I believe I can be better, I will be better. If I believe I can change, I can change.

To become mindful about how we are narrating our stories to ourselves, we need to be convinced that we can do things differently; that it is possible to see things in a different way. We need to believe we can change. To be willing to apply the work of this book, you need to have a growth mindset. You need to believe that change is possible. Your life circumstances are not fixed and your stories can be told in many different ways. You can actively weave the threads of your stories and shape the tapestry of your life. And most interestingly, the way you narrate the stories of your life circumstances has a significant impact on your perception of your life, its potential and the way in which you live. It makes sense not to tell ourselves our stories in ways that emerge out of habit. If we are mindful about how we tell ourselves our stories and we are deliberate about the way in which we tell our stories to ourselves, we are choosing the way we live. We are weaving our own tapestry.

If you are willing to take control of your life, to see the word 'live' as a very active verb and not some kind of passively experienced existence... If you want to weave your own life tapestry, and make it a masterpiece, read on!

In the pages that follow, the story elements are broken down so that you can become more intimately acquainted with the ways in which the stories unfold. We begin with the conflict of the story.

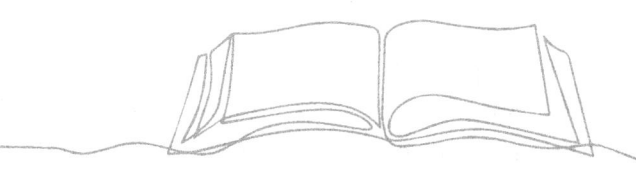

Identifying the conflict and complications

The conflict is the main problem of a story – it is the thing that is causing all the problems, the thing that needs to be resolved. Complications are the story events that occur because this conflict exists. Each of the seven narratives has a particular conflict central to the storyline; a main problem that needs to be overcome. It is what is behind all of the events that occur along the way. In our lives, these are the problems that we face. These can be large or small; they can be broadly impacting or just one of your own personal annoyances. For example, the conflict may be world poverty or it may be that the kids have left a Lego on the floor in the lounge room, which of course you have stepped on... with bare feet. Big or small, broad or narrow, each then has a flow on effect – the complications. Continuing the Lego narrative, you may then shout at the kids. You may end up with a migraine. You may end up having a row with your partner because of the foul mood that torturous piece of Lego has engendered. These are the events of your life that occur as a result of the conflict.

We can unpick the threads of each narrative and identify their conflict and the nature of the complications. When you are familiar with the conflicts of the seven narratives, you will be able to recognise the stories that you are telling yourself. You will see very clearly how you are telling your story. This will also provide you with six other ideas for how you could potentially be telling yourself the story.

Your toolbox starts here. Read about each conflict below and become intimately familiar.

Overcoming the monster

When we are in a situation having to overcome the monster, the conflict is between us and something big. The 'something' seems overwhelming. It is greater than us. It has power we don't see ourselves as possessing. We are much smaller and less powerful than this thing. We have to defeat this force, built up by ourselves to appear monstrous and undefeatable, and the task to overcome the monster is enormous. Our complications may be to do with recognising the thing we are dealing with as a monster and the ways in which it is affecting our lives. We may be focused on working out ways we can defeat it.

Rags to riches

When we are in a rags to riches narrative, we are unseen. We are overlooked. We are potentially treated poorly and in some way suffering. We believe we have all the characteristics, skills, ability and so forth required to have all that we desire but we are experiencing a powerlessness to have these traits revealed. Our plot unfolds with us staying true to ourselves, holding firm to our values and maintaining our hard work while dealing with the hardship of feeling or being oppressed and not being recognised for what we have to offer.

The quest

There is an overarching goal we have when we are narrating through the quest plot. There is something we want to achieve or have. Maybe it is a place we want to reach. The conflict is in not having or being far from this goal. We face distractions and challenges along the way to achieving this goal. These all contribute to the learning and growth we require; growing our capacity to achieve the bigger goal. We may even have broken down our goal into small chunks that need to be achieved on the journey to the greater goal. We have help along the way and expect this to be a lengthy process – a long-term commitment.

Comedy

It is the confusion surrounding truth that is at the heart of the comedy storyline. This creates all manner of problems and misunderstandings as a result of this hidden reality or truth.

Tragedy

The characters involved in this narrative are fundamentally flawed and will not be able to overcome their flaws in order to resolve the conflict. These flaws keep creating issues for the characters. They may keep trying to resolve their issues or may just keep progressing through life with their flaws getting in the way of progress, success or a positive outcome. Alternatively, in this plot, we are absolutely powerless to change some circumstance where things are not turning out for us no matter what we do. It is the situation that is flawed and the situation creates ongoing problems.

Rebirth

If our story is a rebirth, the problem lies within ourselves. There is some change we require, something we need to learn or adjust within ourselves to move forward and to have a better life. Complications arise for us while we remain unchanged or the changes are not extreme enough for them to have a positive impact on our life or the situation we are in.

Journey and return

Our world is changed or is in some way unfamiliar. We are uncomfortable. This discomfort within the different situation causes issues for us. Complications are to do with the discomfort, the learning we are acquiring and our adjustment to our new environment.

HOW DOES KNOWING WHAT THE CONFLICT IS IN THE STORY HELP ME?

A conscious awareness of the conflict in the story, and how it gives rise to complications in our lives, makes the narratives far more recognisable to us. When we are reflecting on our stories, we can look for these conflicts and complications to help us identify which of the seven stories is in play. This lays out our narrative for us and gives us clarity.

When we see our current narrative so clearly, we can also use this information to guide us in how to tell the story to ourselves in other ways. We can try using other narratives to tell our stories to ourselves. We can reflect on how these other stories make us feel and then decide which will serve us best.

Before we can make the best choice, though, we need to know how each story ends. The resolution of the story is the pathway to solving the conflict. When we know this, we know the direction we need to take.

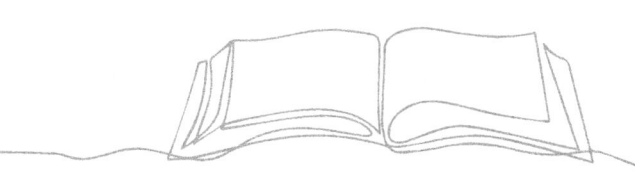

Seeking resolution

Each of the narratives has a particular way in which the story ends or a pathway to resolution. This is part of the elemental structure of the story and our brain is wired to expect that the story will take this path. When we recognise the narrative we are telling, we will be able to see the direction our story is taking. Knowing how we expect the story to resolve offers insight into how we can work to address the situation in our life. The resolution gives a general idea of what must be done and then we need to work out the specifics according to the circumstances we are experiencing.

If we are telling our story as an overcoming of the monster, we know we are going to have to fight for what we want or believe in. There will be a clash or challenge that requires us to pit ourselves against the perceived greater force in some way. We will need to bring all of our strength, cunning, skill and ingenuity to the fray to achieve our goal. This is a win-lose outcome.

If it is a rags to riches story, we need to stay true to ourselves. We also need to knuckle down to the hard graft and put up with some injustice or unfairness because eventually we will be recognised for our efforts, skills or attributes. Our exceptional nature needs to be noticed by a key person or people. Our innate qualities need to be uncovered for us to receive our just reward. We must remain hopeful that others will see us for who we are. We may need to use our own skill or wits to have our beauty, attribute or skill revealed. We may have someone around who can actually help this happen; a champion to our cause.

If it is a quest, we will need to be committed to applying our skill, ingenuity, strength and ability over and over. We will need to focus on achieving a host of goals and experiencing learning and growth, building our skills and capacity through these. Then comes the final overcoming and attainment of our ultimate goal.

If the story is a comedy, the players within the story need to come to some kind of understanding, truth needs to be revealed or some confusion needs to be cleared. This may be something you can take an active role in helping to happen, either directly or indirectly, to achieve the ending you desire.

If this story is a tragedy, we are going to have to lament the loss or ending of something with regret, potentially, and understand that nothing can be done. We then can move on.

If this is a rebirth, then you are going to have to look inside of you, do some work on yourself, and make some kind of internal change that is going to help you in the situation you find yourself. If things aren't changing for you (if you are not getting the outcome you seek) do more, go harder or do something different.

If we are telling the story of a journey and return, we need to be prepared to learn something, to develop some skills and character that will help us to cope with this new world or change in our environment. We need to be curious and open to this learning – ready to make the adjustments required. We then need to be prepared to apply the learning when we return to our old environment or our normal existence, making our lives better.

HOW DOES KNOWING THE RESOLUTION OF EACH STORY HELP ME?

We crave the ending to stories that we are familiar with and that fit the narrative. We cannot escape this wiring. We will want this ending even if we are unaware of it. When we are explicitly clear about what pathway we crave for our narratives we can look at the situation we are in and determine how we can move forward. These story resolutions give us a guideline which helps us find resolution for the circumstances of our lives. To move forward, we will need to reflect on our own situation and determine the specifics of how we may proceed.

If the pathway forward does not feel right or you can't see how it would work for you, then perhaps you are not applying the narrative that is right for you. It is worth reflecting on this and trying out other narratives for size.

There are many ways in which the narratives can do us a service or disservice. We need to be very aware of the impact of our narration so we can choose those stories that serve us.

To serve or to hinder, that is the question

No one story has particular value over any other. No one story is inherently a better choice for us in how we recount these times of our lives. Each can potentially serve us through the narrative or hinder us somehow. What follows are some generic circumstances in which the plots can help us or hold us back. Any of these may apply at any time but probably not all.

We need to examine the unique circumstances we are facing and decide for ourselves whether the narrative we are telling serves us or otherwise.

OVERCOMING THE MONSTER

All you have to do to diminish your fear is to develop more trust in your ability to handle whatever comes your way. **(Jeffers, 1987, p.16)**

Serves us when:
- We can convince ourselves we have the capacity to defeat this thing.
- We believe we can do this.

- We are prepared to prepare for the stoush; we will put the work in that we need to.
- When it can provide us with a peak experience: that 'heightened sense of wonder, awe, or ecstasy over an experience.' (Bonaiuto, 2016)
- We are feeling strong, capable and courageous or particularly clever.
- We have the tools at our disposal.
- When we can keep our eyes focused on the prize, the positive outcome or the overcoming.
- It is okay to have a win-lose outcome.
- We are going to win.
- When we have conviction in our morals; we are 'in the right'.

Does not serve us when:

- We don't see ourselves as being able to defeat the monster no matter what we try.
- We feel weak and poorly equipped.
- One opportunity to face this will lead to a failure that we will not recover from.
- The situation is a marathon and not a sprint.
- We are ground down by the experience.
- It is not okay to have a win-lose outcome.
- We are going to lose.

RAGS TO RICHES

Start unknown, finish unforgettable. - **Misty Copeland**

Serves us when:

- We know that the hard work we are putting in will actually result in a reward.
- When we have conviction in our morals; we are 'in the right'.
- We really do have the skills, attributes and abilities required and we know it.
- When taking a more aggressive approach to resolving the issue is not going to achieve the ultimate aim.
- Our hope has the potential to be translated into reality.
- We can use our wits or skill to reveal a previously hidden or only glimpsed ability, skill or attribute.
- There may be someone 'on our side' who is working to have us acknowledged.

Does not serve us when:

- We do not get the expected reward for our hard work or application.
- The oppressive forces are harmful to us and we simply put up with it.

- We hold on to false hope.
- We are not prepared to try to gain recognition or to elicit help in this regard.
- It is taking too long.
- We fall into the trap of 'I will be happy when...' thinking.

THE QUEST

...repeated victories over your problems are the rungs on your ladder of success. With each victory you grow in wisdom, stature and experience. You become a better, bigger, more successful person each time you meet a problem and conquer it...
(Hill and Stone, p.69)

Serves us when:
- There is a clear goal that all this is leading toward.
- The success is expected to be a marathon and not a sprint.
- We can draw on the strengths of others to help us achieve our goals.
- Each individual success builds our self-concept and skill set in preparation for the final overcoming or achievement.

Does not serve us when:
- There is no clear goal or reward other than overcoming adversity; we have nothing 'bigger' to work toward.
- We never get to the goal.
- We completely lose sight of the goal.
- We lack stamina for the long game.
- We insist on acting alone, not taking the help that is available to us.

COMEDY

When a thing is funny, search it carefully for a hidden truth. - **George Bernard Shaw**

Three things cannot long be hidden; the sun, the moon and the truth. - **Confucius**

Serves us when:
- Seeing things as ironic, absurd or comical takes the power out of the situation.
- We are dealing with a situation where we know that there are some truths to be revealed for everyone to see the situation for what it is.
- When we have conviction in our morals.
- When we have faith that the truth will be revealed.
- When we can assist in making people aware of the truth.

Does not serve us when:
- We fall into the trap of being passive and shaking our heads at our own folly and that of others.
- We are not being active enough.
- We are not taking things seriously enough.
- We become too frustrated with the state of confusion caused by the unseen truths and absurdity.
- We fall into the trap of 'I will be happy when...' thinking.
- We think that uncovering truths and resolving confusion means everything will turn out well in the end without any further work on our own behalf. Happy ever after is a falsehood – it is not something that just happens. It requires effort to maintain a happy status quo.

TRAGEDY

I am not what happened to me, I am what I choose to become. - **Carl Jung**

Serves us when:
- We need to let go of something in our lives.
- We have no agency in the situation or the outcome. There is nothing we can do and we are prepared to let it go.
- We have done everything we possibly can and there is nothing left but to let it go.

- It is someone else's story and we cannot do anything to help.

Does not serve us when:
- We have more work to do before we quit this thing. We haven't tried everything.
- We spend too long mourning for what we have lost and don't use this as an opportunity to put these things behind us. Helen Keller said, 'When one door of happiness closes, another opens; but often we look so long at the closed door that we do not see the one which has been opened for us.'
- The narrative is unfinished and may turn out differently if we give it time.
- We have a habit of quitting.

REBIRTH

When you blame any outside force for any of your experience of life, you are literally giving away all your power. - **Susan Jeffers**

Serves us when:
- We are in a situation where effecting some change in ourselves will result in positive changes in our lives.
- When having faith in the journey of discovering and changing infuses us with a positivity about the process and commits us to the outcome.

- We are willing to see that we need to change.
- We are willing to work on ourselves.
- We can see when things are working and when they are not.
- We are ground zero for the issue.

Does not serve us when:
- We have an unrealistic belief that someone in our lives will change if we just...
- When we are seeing that if someone just changed everything would be better but they are unwilling to change. It is not your story!
- When we have a tendency to take responsibility where it is not due.
- We are trapped in believing we are right about the change we think we need to effect but are not. As Jesse Potter said, 'If you always do what you've always done, you always get what you've always gotten.'

JOURNEY AND RETURN

Things do not change; we change. - **Henry David Thoreau**

The journey is the treasure. - **Lloyd Alexander**

Serves us when:

- We can see that this experience that we are having will help us to grow.
- We are benefiting from this immersion in uncomfortable territory.
- We can see how we might apply the learning we are gaining in our lives beyond this experience.

Does not serve us when:

- We will put up with things because we have convinced ourselves it is good for us or will help us to grow.
- We are not open to the learning available to us on this journey.

HOW DOES IT HELP ME KNOWING HOW EACH NARRATIVE CAN GENERICALLY SERVE ME (OR NOT)?

Having this information laid out for us gives us the opportunity to see things we may otherwise not recognise. And when we know the common ways in which each narrative may be appropriate or inappropriate in our circumstances, we then have some go-to ideas to reflect on our thinking and feelings.

We can question: 'are these my thoughts and feelings?'

If your answer is 'yes,' to any of the ways in which a narrative *doesn't serve us*, then we need to move away from using that narrative to tell the story.

If we can answer 'yes,' to any of the ways in which each narrative may *serve us*, these are your 'go-to' choices for the best narrative to use in telling your story to yourself.

If you are trapped in the nightmare stage of any of the narratives, then you can be sure that this narrative is not serving you. This can be revealed by a need for escapism, to self-medicate to cope with your circumstances or a tendency to ruminate – to be thinking about the problem over and over again while wanting to talk about how bad things are. This is a red flag that your narrative is not serving you. It is definitely time to change the narrative. Alternatively, you may need to adjust your narration within the narrative you are telling.

Adjusting the telling *within* the narrative to make it serve you

Sometimes we are using the right narrative to tell our story but it is still not serving us. Take John's recent experience as an example.

JOHN RAILS AGAINST THE LOCKDOWN

For pete's sake, why are we going in to lock down? Another week of lost income. I can't go for a ride without a mask and can't stand those things on my face. I haven't even got one anyway so no walking the dog. This is crap. It's not like this is going to make any difference. The whole thing is bollocks!

There had been a breakout of the coronavirus, a case of community spreading, for the first time in the whole COVID-19 thing in our state. Our politicians have acted decisively, determining that if we all stay home for five days we can get this under control. Unfortunately for John, he works with clients at his house. We are not allowed to have visitors come to our home and therefore his current income generating activity is curtailed. John is very angry and his emotions have taken hold. He has nothing good to say and nothing good to think.

YES, IT IS A MONSTER

This situation is definitely a monster. The issue of this virus is massive. To date there have been 103.5 million cases of the virus in the world. More than two million people have lost their lives in one year and everyone has their own cross to bear in dealing with this thing. John has some significant challenges. His income is dependent on people being able to utilise his services in a face-to-face situation.

But John is heavily immersed in the nightmare stage of this narrative. He is overwhelmed by the problems and only sees one solution – that we don't go into lockdown at all. I think that whilst the narrative is probably the most relevant in this situation, if John could adjust his telling and look at his arsenal a little more closely, he may emerge the victor from this fight.

CHOOSE YOUR OWN ADVENTURE

John has a couple of pathways open to him. He can shout, fight and be cranky about this thing and how it is affecting his livelihood. The reality is, this action will not advance his cause. If his aim in defeating the monster is to reverse the lockdown decision so he can keep working, the narrative is not serving him. He cannot win.

Alternatively, he can think of this as an opportunity to sharpen his axe.

Give me six hours to chop down a tree and I will spend four sharpening the axe. - **Abraham Lincoln**

John can spend this time doing all those things he doesn't have time for when his working week is filled with servicing clients or recovering from doing just that! He can explore ways of growing his business and working smarter, not harder. He can spend some time on exploring the passive income streams he so often talks about. He can use this time to spark his creativity – something he finds hard when he is tired from working face-to-face with people. If he remains open-minded about this situation and solutions-focused, the opportunity provided by this monster can have him spending those four hours sharpening his axe and when he can get back into the fray he will be well placed to be going better, smarter, harder and faster than ever before.

His choice.

HOW CAN CHANGING WITHIN THE NARRATIVE SERVE ME

Sometimes the narrative we are telling is the right one, we are just not telling it to ourselves in ways that serve us. When we explore whether the narrative is serving us, it is usually proven quickly by looking at how we are feeling about our stories and whether we are finding satisfactory resolution. If not, we can think about different ways of telling, be reflective and try to reframe. This might be about how we are perceiving the characters or the events. It may also be about the pathway to resolution.

In the case of overcoming the monster, the mode of fighting can be very varied. We can be pugilistic and argumentative, or we can be wily and make our mode of fighting work for us, as in the story of John above.

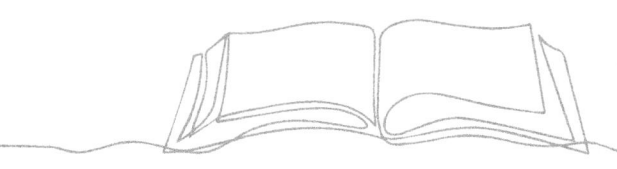

Having conviction in our morals, being 'in the right': the key to deserving a reward

Sometimes there are what Booker calls 'dark versions' of our narratives. In these versions, the narrative contains characters whose very character or aims are not honourable and therefore they cannot have the resolution that is expected of the kind-hearted or those characters with clear consciences. The narrative structures are there but these characters cannot be rewarded in the plot. This is something else that is hard wired into us. These are our fundamental expectations for the progression of the narrative.

And we are the heroes or protagonists in our own stories.

If we expect to truly believe we deserve the positive ending in the narrative as its protagonist, we need to make sure that we feel deserving of the ending we desire. In order to do that we need to have a clear conscience. We need to have conviction in our own morals. We need to feel like we are 'in the right'.

How do we do this?

We can tell ourselves 'I am enough' all we like, but we also need to make sure we have a clear set of beliefs and values or morals that we are ascribing to in the narratives of our lives. If the decisions we make and the behaviours we live out are in keeping with our core values, then we will feel deserving of the outcomes we seek in the situation. Then, and only then, will we actually 'be enough'.

Our values are what we know to be good and right. We need to identify our values and make sure we are living up to them in our actions. Be clear on what we believe in and live by it every single day. As Tony Robbins says, 'There is power in individuals who congruently lead lives where their philosophies and actions are one,' (Robbins, p.343). And, 'Only living and doing what you believe is the "right thing" will give you that sense of inner strength that we all deserve.' **(Robbins, p.345)**.

I have been thinking about my own values.
Here is the list as it stands:

Contribution	- To add value to every situation in which I find myself.
	- To make my friends, family and colleagues feel like they have value, that they are enough.
Joyous	- To bring joy to life.
Industrious	- To work hard.
Integrity	- My words match my deeds – honesty in dealings.

Success	- To achieve success in my professional life.
Justice	- For things to be fair and reasonable.
Do no harm	- In all the dealings that I have, in every aspect of my existence, I wish to cause no harm to others.

I have also reflected on how I am living up to these values. I have had to think deeply to find an example of where I am not living up to my values. This is not because I am in any way flawless, just blind to myself unless I am choosing to be mindful. Don't worry, I found one!

I once worked with someone who is a very 'difficult' character. Although she has many excellent qualities she was abrasive, spoke negatively quite often and drew her team together with negative cohesion. This person created a lot of conflict in the workplace. People did not want to work with her. She judged others and made her judgements public. And I was her leader. Others looked to me to 'solve' this problem or simply to share their frustrations.

On occasion, I caught myself being uncharitable in the instance of this sharing. My own prejudices in terms of how I felt about this person and her impact on me, my reaction to her behaviours in relation to my values, have meant that I have occasionally joined in the complaining (or 'bitching') about her behaviour.

And when I did this, I did not feel good about myself.

I can do all the justifying in the world about the kind of person that she was and how she had earned this negative talk. But it still didn't sit well with me. Why?

It didn't sit well with me because it goes against my value system. It contradicts my belief that I should 'do no harm', to make a contribution to the environment that I am in and to act with integrity. Whilst I was contributing to the negative talk about this person I was not helping anyone to come to terms with their feelings about her behaviour. I was not in any way dealing positively with my own feelings. I was driving the negativity in the environment around this person. I was not acting in a way that I think is appropriate – speaking positively and acting in ways that improve my surrounds. I was not acting with integrity.

It doesn't matter how big, bad or ugly the monster is, I still needed to act with integrity to feel I earned the right to be the victor in this narrative.

I resolved to change. Once I made this resolution, I felt a weight was lifted. I was no longer the flawed character undeserving of a positive outcome. I had the conviction of my morals (or at least I would earn it back with new behaviours that fit with my moral code). I intended, then, to endow those who complained with a listening ear but also some strategies to help them deal with their feelings about this person's behaviour. I also resolved to go to the source and work with this person to ensure that she embarked on a process of change. My strategy as a leader has been to treat people as if they already have the characteristics and behaviours that I want to see them display. I verbally admire them for demonstrating these behaviours and watch them grow into that reputation. I also prefer to model best practice. That was my plan for this person going forward. I would be true to myself, conducting myself according to my values.

Once I found my moral compass and was behaving in congruence with my values, I felt justified in taking action and working to shift this colleague in her behaviour.

Be mindful- it is not enough to know your values and live by them. You also need to feel that they are 'high values'. These need to be values that we are proud of and feel good about. Selfishness and hedonism are certainly values but you may have trouble justifying these beliefs to your higher self. In this case, you will need to work on changing your values or reordering them so that the values that we would consider less desirable are not the ones we are prioritising in our everyday behaviours.

Alternatively, when we live out these behaviours, we do them in ways that support other well-thought-of values. For example, if we are concurrently hedonistic and value contributing, we may choose to organise a gala event that brings many people together to dance and enjoy themselves while making charitable contributions. If we value ourselves, and we value industry, we can lift weights for an hour each day in order to grow our health and strength.

Changing our behaviour is merely a matter of having a value in the forefront of our minds in our daily dealings. We need to train ourselves. We need to consider our decisions and actions in relation to that value and ensure that what we are thinking, saying and doing is in keeping with our values. We do this over time until we remain in keeping with that value unconsciously.

Being true to your core values involves a lifelong journey of discovering, experimentation, trial, and error. **(Christian)**

When we are acting congruently with our values, we have conviction in our morals. We believe we are doing the right thing. And when we are the protagonist in the stories we tell ourselves, and we hold the conviction of our morals, we feel deserving of the goal or ending we seek from the narrative.

Nothing in life can match the fulfilment of knowing you've done what you truly believe is the right thing. **(Robbins, p.368)**

Spend some time identifying your values. What follows is a list of values that may help you.

Consider your behaviours and decisions over the next period of time and decide if the list you have identified is truly 'you' and whether you are living up to your values system. If you truly value these things and have not lived up to them, train yourself to do so. Be deserving of being the winner in the narrative!

Having conviction in our morals, being 'in the right': the key to deserving a reward

- Abundance
- Authenticity
- Achievement
- Adventure
- Authority
- Autonomy
- Balance
- Beauty
- Boldness
- Challenge
- Change
- Citizenship
- Community
- Compassion
- Competency
- Connection
- Consistency
- Contribution
- Courage
- Creativity
- Curiosity
- Dependability
- Determination
- Diversity
- Do no harm
- Education
- Efficiency
- Entrepreneurialism
- Environmentalism
- Excellence
- Fairness
- Faith
- Fame
- Family
- Fitness
- Forgiveness
- Freedom
- Friendships
- Fun
- Generosity
- Good humour
- Gratitude
- Growth
- Happiness
- Harmony
- Honesty
- Humanity
- Humour
- Industry
- Influence
- Inner Harmony
- Integrity
- Intelligence
- Joy
- Justice
- Kindness
- Knowledge
- Leadership

- Learning
- Love
- Loyalty
- Meaningful Work
- Open-mindedness
- Openness
- Optimism
- Passion
- Patriotism
- Peace
- Perseverance
- Pleasure
- Poise
- Popularity
- Positivity
- Power
- Prosperity
- Quality
- Reciprocity
- Recognition
- Reliability
- Religion
- Reputation
- Respect
- Responsibility
- Security
- Self-Respect
- Service
- Spirituality
- Stability
- Success
- Status
- Teamwork
- Trustworthiness
- Wealth
- Wellness
- Wisdom

HOW CAN 'HAVING CONVICTION IN MY MORALS' HELP ME?

We are programmed to want the protagonist to be successful in a narrative except in darker versions of the stories. In these darker versions, the hero has flaws and lacks an appropriate moral code. We must be mindful that we are not shaping ourselves as flawed characters and thus situating ourselves as undeserving of the reward in the plots we are shaping. If we do the work of defining our own values systems and ensuring we live up to them, we can also be sure that we feel that we deserve to be rewarded in the plots that we use to narrate our lives.

Integrity is doing the right thing even when no one is watching. - **CS Lewis**

And an additional benefit of having a clear moral code that we believe contains high values and we live up to every day is that we will always feel 'good enough'.

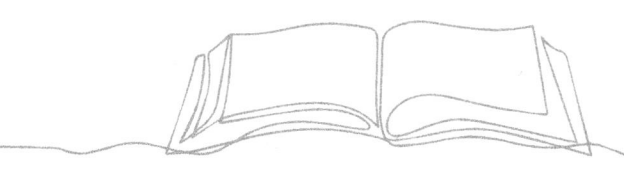

Your superpowers: visualisation and affirmations

If we want to change the way we are narrating our stories so that they serve us we must recognise what will actually serve us. To determine which narrative is the one that is most beneficial we need to immerse ourselves in the visualisation of different versions of the story, testing out the storylines in our imaginations, sensing in our inner selves how it makes us feel. If we can familiarise ourselves with the story elements and have a go at restructuring our story (trying to make it fit a different storyline) and see how that storyline feels to us, we are well on the way to working out what plot is going to serve us in this experience of our lives. If we can imagine ourselves living out the narrative according to the plot that best serves us, we are further along the road to self-determination, feeling in control and living our best lives.

Visualisation is a powerful technique and has been long recognised as the strategy of champions. Covey references the work of Dr Charles Garfield when he says, 'peak performers are visualisers. They see it; they feel it; they experience it before they actually do it,' (p.134). Some of our greatest athletes use visualisation techniques to achieve their goals in sport. But it is not only limited to athletes. Peak performers in life can use this strategy.

When I was preparing for my first formal public speaking event, I was nervous about the outcomes. I went through a visualisation process multiple times. Sometimes I would visualise myself running through my whole speech. Other times I would see myself in parts. In every visual iteration the imagery was of a successful public speaking event. The event lived up to my visualisations and more.

Jay Shetty talks about the power of visualisation: 'In order to create something, we have to imagine it. This is why visualisation is important. Whatever we build internally can be built externally' (pp.197-8). If we want to create the world of our choosing, we need to first imagine it. This is further confirmed by Vilhauer, 'It is impossible to create something that cannot first be imagined.' All creators, designers or inventors have a mental image of their creations prior to putting plans on paper or making a model. Likewise, we can and do imagine our lives – what has come before and what is yet to come. Thus, we can be the creators of our lives.

Be careful: our brains are always visualising things, imagining events, picturing our stories. These are very powerful. We should be directing our brains to visualise the stories of our lives in ways that serve us; being in control of our thoughts and visualisations and not just experiencing the whim of our active brains! A timely reminder: live consciously.

VISUALISATION TECHNIQUE

In order to visualise yourself living out a new narrative, be very clear in your mind how you want the events to play out. Know who the characters are and imagine conversations, locations, facial expressions.

Take yourself deeper, into the feelings of the event. Imagine how you would feel if things were unfolding the way you desired. In fact, once you start imagining this, the feelings often come naturally. Deepen these feelings, feel them as if you were there.

See the events unfold according to the narrative that serves you. Your emotions should be positive, empowering, good. If these are not the feelings you experience, explore a new narrative or a new pathway forward within your narrative until the feelings are 'right'.

Repeat this visualisation technique until your thoughts become your reality.

THE POWER OF AFFIRMATIONS

Affirmations are positive statements that support visualisation by giving us the self-belief that we can make things happen. They convince our brains that things ARE the way the affirmation says they are and then we subconsciously go about closing the gap between the affirmation and reality.

Affirmations have the capacity to instil in us confidence and self-belief. They can reduce stress and focus us positively to cope with what life throws at us. As the folks at Mind Tools tell us: 'spending just a few minutes thinking about your best qualities... can calm your nerves, increase your confidence, and improve your chances of a successful outcome.' This can be applied to all aspects of our lives and certainly has an application in how we tell stories to ourselves. According to Moore, 'When we are able to deal with negative messages and replace them with positive statements, we can construct more adaptive, hopeful narratives about who we are and what we can accomplish.'

Affirmations are constructed employing positive language. They should always be in present tense and be believable and achievable for us.

Some examples of affirmations include:
- I decide how I feel.
- I choose my own narrative.
- My life is my own, I am free to choose my path.
- My story is mine to tell. I make my choices deliberately and consciously.

Some affirmations are highly suited to particular narratives, empowering us to cope with our circumstances and/or move toward resolution. Here are some examples of powerful affirmations that suit each narrative:

Overcoming the monster
- I am strong, powerful and capable.
- I am fearless and brave.

Rags to riches
- I am respected and valued.
- I am talented and capable.

The quest
- I am bold and take action.
- I keep going.

Comedy
- Doors to truth and love are opening for me.
- Being myself is my ultimate truth. I am myself freely and without inhibition.

Tragedy
- This too shall pass.
- I am a survivor.

Rebirth
- I am changing for the better.
- Every day, in every way, I am becoming better and better.

Journey and return
- Every experience is a lesson or a blessing.
- Any adversity is an opportunity to grow.

If we want to power up our ability to change our narrative or control our circumstance, we can add affirmations to our daily routine. Covey describes affirmations as 'extremely powerful in rescripting' (p.134). These will give us the mindset that will have us working actively, both consciously and subconsciously, to make our desired narratives a reality. And according to our friends at Mind Tools, affirmations and visualisation can be used concurrently for some power ups; 'affirmations work particularly well alongside visualisation. So, instead of just picturing the change you would like to see, you can also write it down or say it out loud using a positive affirmation.' Use affirmations to strengthen your work in achieving effective change.

And repetition is key. If we want our brains to take on this reprogramming, we need to repeat our affirmations to ourselves until they become our firm belief.

HOW CAN VISUALISING AND AFFIRMING HELP ME?

Visualisation helps us to see how our lives were, are or might be when we play out a narrative in our imagination. It gives us the opportunity to try out alternatives – try before we buy! In addition to that, visualisation can help us to rescript our lives into the new narrative.

Affirmations are the supercharge strategy to make it all happen. Affirmations help us to feel empowered in the narrative. They set our mindset for success and positive self-belief.

It makes sense, then, to visualise and use affirmations to choose and then cement a new narrative. This will allow us to choose the surest path to being able to cope with our circumstances or find our way to a resolution. This will give us clarity and conviction that we are on the right path. This will help us to live consciously and to be in contrcl of our lives.

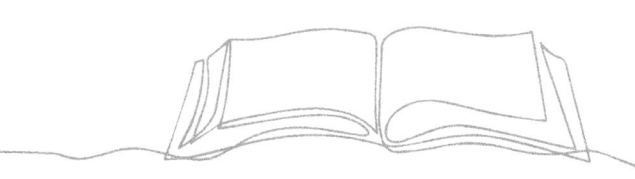

Journaling

Be certain to use two of the greatest, yet simplest working tools ever invented – tools used by a genius such as Thomas Edison – a pencil and a piece of paper. **(Hill, p.131)**

It has been long recognised that journaling is an effective therapy tool,

Journaling is an incredibly beneficial self-care technique, which doesn't just enhance feelings of happiness, but reduces stress, clarifies thoughts and feelings, and ultimately helps you get to know yourself better. **(Bennett)**

Many 'achievers' and well-grounded people use a morning routine where journaling forms a significant portion. Others find night times before bed a useful time. If using this technique, you will need to work out the 'when' that suits you best.

Journaling gives us the chance to 'listen' to ourselves telling our stories. If you write things down freely in a journal, you can then have the opportunity to look at it dispassionately at a later point, either straight after writing or at a time when you can pull the feelings out of the experience and look at the words unemotionally, or from the point of view of a caring friend. From this perspective, it is easier to observe the presence of the narratives and to explore alternatives.

Inspiration for using a journaling process has come to me from a blog by Taylor Bennett (2018). I have outlined my process below. You can use this to help you analyse your thinking and apply the theory of the Seven Stories; work out which narrative you are defaulting to as well as the narrative that will most serve you.

JOURNALING PROCESS

Free write

Take some time to simply put down your thoughts. Write anything that comes into your head. Tease out something that is concerning you; be it the housework, the children's achievement, your relationship, a work situation. Hone in on the concern and write more deeply about it.

Take a break

Step away from the writing for a period of time; make a cuppa, do a chore, hug the kids, go for a walk, leave it for a day, a week. When you come back to the writing you will want some distance from the emotion that you were investing into the situation. The break gives you some distance.

Review the writing

Read back what you have written. Make sure you don't dive straight back into the emotions that you have about the issue (meditation and box breathing may help – these strategies are explained later). Characterise yourself in this reading process as a compassionate friend – care but don't be immersed in the feelings. Treat the situation as someone else's experience.

Look for the narratives

Review the narrative structures. See if you can find evidence of them in your telling. Quite often you cannot. This is okay. If you go back to section three, where the stories of people's experiences are recorded, you will find little evidence of the seven plot lines in the first telling. I have overlaid these after having been told of the events. In this case, you may start to ponder which of the narratives might work for the telling of your story.

Retell your story using the narratives

Your next step is to look at how you might tell your story using the different plotlines. Try rewriting the story using as many of the alternatives as possible. Use the section on conflict and complications to assist.

Determine whether this telling serves you

Go back to the section in part four where we explore the generic consequences of each storyline. Explore how they apply to your personal circumstances. Write these down.

Work out which one is the right one for your telling

As you are rewriting the story (or afterwards in reading the alternatives) re-immerse yourself in the emotion of the story. Visualise. Really feel the weight of the experience within yourself. Make sure you shake off the emotion of the last story before immersing yourself into the next retelling so you are clear where the feelings belong. A breathing technique can support this if you are finding it difficult to remove yourself from the emotion (again, see box breathing and meditation). It should become very clear to you when the 'right' telling presents itself. You should feel aligned, empowered and a sense of rightness about the telling.

Look for your pathway to resolution

Review the pathways to resolution in this section of the book. Hone in on the one that matches the 'right' telling of your story. It gives you an outline of what needs to be done in order to resolve your conflict. Write about this, exploring your circumstances and imagine how the problem might be resolved along those lines. You may find it useful to think of two or three ways in which this may be able to be resolved whilst maintaining the same plotline. If you are having trouble with this, bring a trusted friend into the conversation and see what they think. Keep them on track with the pathway you know is right for you – don't let them retell YOUR story when you ask for their help! You have been through a process to identify what you know is right for you, not what is right for them.

Keep writing

Just because you have analysed your situation, defined your narrative and determined a pathway forward, doesn't mean your work here is done! There may come a time when the narrative being told in this way no longer serves you. You can see from the examples in *Part Four* that some of them are a one-moment process of determining the narrative that suits whilst others are a journey of discovery throughout which the narrative changes over time. Continuing to journal your journey will help you to think clearly about what is happening for you and if your narrative is still serving you or whether you need to rethink and reframe. This is how life progresses and how we maintain control of the events in our lives.

Charles Duhigg (2012) described journaling as a keystone habit. In a study on weight loss, journaling created a habit of mindfulness that resulted in the subjects achieving their goals. We can utilise this keystone habit to transform our lives by applying the process outlined above.

The most influential aspect of this practice for me has been in pulling myself out of the immersion in the experience. Taking that step back and looking at it all without emotion. Looking for the plot line has allowed me to remove myself from the situation and see it from the outside. This is amazingly empowering. If you find it difficult to remove the emotion from the experience, try physically removing yourself from the task for a while. Take one of the breaks described above. Meditation and breathing techniques as outlined in the next few pages are also powerful 're-setters'.

HOW CAN JOURNALING HELP ME?

The importance of journaling is in chronicling your thought processes and being clearly aware of how you are thinking; of the narratives at play; of the choices available for how you frame your life experiences and the consequences of those choices. Journaling gives us the capacity to decide, to make clear choices with all of the options and consequences laid out for us. It helps us to be mindful of how we are thinking, the decisions we are making. Journaling puts us in the driver's seat and gives us the power to be in control of our lives.

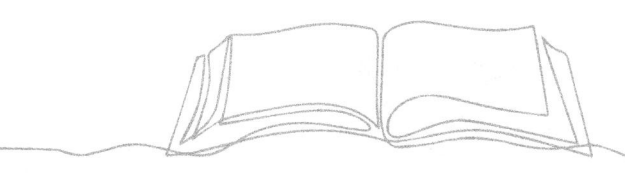

Success elixir #1: Box breathing

When we immerse ourselves in our problems and really mull them over as we have done in the journaling process or in visualisation, we are encouraging the body's stress response. Our body does not know that we are not in an event that requires a fight/flight response. It reacts exactly as if it is. When we think deeply and ruminate on our problems, when we make ourselves feel the emotion of the event, we are invoking the release of hormones that summon that response. We are putting our bodies under stress.

> *In fight-or-flight mode, the body feels threatened and reacts to help the person escape or avoid a threatening situation. Among other things, the body releases hormones to make the heart beat faster, breathing to quicken, and to boost blood sugar levels.* **(Stinson)**

When we have our bodies experiencing the stress response for too long, there are costs to our health. This is the last thing we want to occur as a result of the process of sorting our lives out! I encourage the use of a breathing technique that will, instead, induce the relaxation response in the body and reverse the effects of the stress response.

There are many breathing techniques that can be used to settle our minds and release us from the stress response. Box breathing is the technique I am sharing with you. You will be amazed when you try this, if you haven't yet, to feel the change in your body when the relaxation response is triggered. Total happy time!

Box breathing

Make yourself comfortable. Sit with your torso straight and your shoulders back. Close your eyes. Breathe in deeply for a count of four. Feel the air fill your stomach, allow your tummy to expand, this allows the lower part of the lungs to fill. Hold the breath for a count of four. Slowly release the breath for a count of four. Wait for a count of four. Repeat. Do this at least three times but if you can do it for several minutes the benefits are far greater.

The feeling of wellbeing is immense from having completed this experience. Try it now!

HOW CAN BOX BREATHING HELP ME?

Box breathing can reverse the stress response and invoke a relaxation response in the body. We may find that we need to do this when we have immersed ourselves in the emotions of retelling or visualising our stories. Box breathing is helpful in restoring our sense of wellbeing.

Success elixir #2: Meditation

Meditation is a powerful technique for reducing stress, inducing the relaxation response and resetting our thoughts. This can be very useful when we find that we cannot see outside of the narrative we are telling; when we are immersed in the feelings of a narrative told in one way and need to step back. It can also help us to reset our feelings when we are visualising a narrative told in a particular way and we are overwhelmed with the feelings it triggers.

> *All human beings have an innate desire to overcome suffering, to find happiness. Training the mind to think differently, through meditation, is one important way to avoid suffering and be happy.*
> **The Dalai Lama**

> **A simple meditation**
>
> - Sit or lie comfortably. I always lay down for meditation. Sitting doesn't make me comfortable!
> - Close your eyes.
> - Breathe naturally.
> - Be consciously aware of your breath. Observe it as you breathe for a while.
> - Shift your focus to the parts of your body, working from the head to the toes. Feel the body part. See its shape. Observe any physical sensations experienced from it. Move to the next part.
> - If a thought comes, allow it. Let it pass and return to the sensations of the body.
> - Do this for a few minutes to start with and build up over time.

HOW CAN MEDITATION HELP ME?

When we go through the practice of immersing ourselves in emotional stories, we are invoking the flight or fight response – we are inducing stress in our bodies. We do not want to leave ourselves feeling these emotions. 'Spending even a few minutes in meditation can restore your calm and inner peace' (Mayo). We may also need to give ourselves strategies to be able to clear the emotions prior to moving on to the next visualisation. Meditation is a portable, free and simple technique that can allow us to release thoughts and feelings and keep us emotionally and physically well.

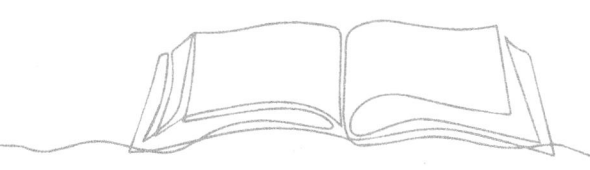

Finding patterns in our narratives

When we take the time to journal our stories or we spend some time reflecting deeply on the stories we tell, patterns can start to emerge. We should be mindful about the patterns within which we tell stories. These, as well, can help or hinder us.

Sometimes we tell the stories favouring a certain plotline. In other times, we evolve in how we tell our stories and we can find patterns there as well.

MONO-PLOTTERS

John has a habit of telling stories where he is overcoming the monster. For example, he has a mother who is problematic. He doesn't like the way his mother treats his father; she is constantly negative, demanding and critical. She has some OCD tendencies which her family find very hard to cope with. He was the guy with the redecorating issue from *Part 3*, also told as an overcoming the monster narrative. In addition to this, John has a recurring medical condition. This overwhelms him and he becomes frustrated and angry – yet another monster in his life.

As John narrates these stories, he shows strong emotions of anger and frustration. He is perpetually engaged in some sort of fight in his life. Is this genuinely healthy for him? Could he tell his stories to himself in ways that are more productive and less draining? For example, his mother could be a fatally flawed human being who he can just accept for who she is, lamenting the tragedy that she will always be annoying and will not live a full life because of her character traits. In this way, he could let the situation go. As explained previously, if he broke his redecorating down into small chunks and celebrated victories instead of grouping the whole thing into one massive monster, he would have tension and release rather than one massive, growing tension. Again, a healthier alternative? And if he maintained his health issue was a monster, go for it, he has now three different narratives running and only one of those would be causing significant stress in his life.

Chris, on the other hand, has the habit of treating many of his life experiences as tragedies. He has cast himself as the flawed main character and is always quite humorous in the telling, for example, when he picked up a prostitute in Bali:

> Chris was working in Bali as a dive instructor. He had finished up his work for the day and was nursing an ice cold Bintang in a local bar. The mood struck him for some company and because he was fully immersed in this digital age, he picked up his phone and started scrolling through his Tinder app. He very quickly hooked a fish, and for most peo-

ple this might be a red flag, but not for our intrepid adventurer. The young lady agreed to meet but refused to come to the location my friend suggested, instead she said she would pick him up on the street. Another flag? Sure enough, she arrived on her scooter, scooped up my friend and whisked him off through a myriad of back streets of Kuta to an out of the way restaurant. This place seemed nice enough and my friend settled in to trying to enjoy the company of this stranger he had just hooked up with on Tinder.

Unfortunately, the pair just could not find their rhythm. It seemed the only common ground they had was availability. They had no common interests and they could not strike up a rapport. He didn't really even find her attractive so flirting was lost to him. Having decided he had had enough, my friend thanked the young lady for her company and made his excuses. Unfortunately for my friend, this instigated something of a scene.

She rose out of her seat and shouted, 'Why you waste my time? You pay me!'

Chris was immediately embarrassed and went to pay his bill. He hadn't realised until that moment he had engaged the services of a hooker. He kept apologising and moved toward the entrance of the restaurant while she shouted at him and issued threats. Chris escaped and hid out for as long as he could in a nearby bar. He was hoping the lady would just go away and that the bodyguard – who she promised in her shouting would be along to extract money from him – was an empty threat. Fortunately for Chris, this was the case!

Chris characterised himself as flawed, having rushed into this date and not done his due diligence in sharing why they were both there that evening: him for a nice time, her for work. As a result, the date failed and Chris put it behind him.

Chris tells his stories of failed relationships where the women are complete nutters. He talks of the business he had and his partners' inappropriate behaviour, leaving him in significant debt.

Chris tells so many of his stories in the frame of a tragedy. He is the central, flawed character. And although he is very humorous in his telling, he has written all of the events/ experiences off as tragedies and put them behind him. He has narrated for himself a history of spectacular failures.

As a result, Chris has a particular expectation around business and patterns around relationships that perpetuate. If he stepped back and observed his narrative, changed his perspective on himself and the way things turn out, perhaps he would be able to tell a different story about his business and relationship success in the future.

THE HAZARDS OF TELLING YOUR STORIES USING A MONO-PLOT

Consider the mono-plot a single mode of storytelling. This may be the overcoming the monster or the rags to riches, or any of the others. But it remains one dimensional, a preference or predilection for a certain telling of your narratives. This can have some negative side effects.

Continuously overcoming the monster

People who tell every story of their life to themselves as an overcoming the monster story are always going to be fighting. They are railing against things – their mother, their boss, their children, opening the jar of jam. This has the potential for leaving the person in stress response constantly as they deal with feelings of frustration and anger. Long-term, facing monsters all the time without feeling empowered to overcome, can impact mental wellness.

Always a Cinderella

If we are perpetually telling ourselves rags to riches stories, we may see ourselves as having wonderful qualities but others fail to see them as we toil under oppressive forces. In this plotline, we might be putting up with an abusive partner, dealing with a work situation where we feel we deserve a raise or promotion and our boss is not recognising the effort we are putting in, or we may have an amazing skill or talent such as art and assume that artists don't realise their true value until they are dead. Whilst the rags to riches story has some hope embedded within the narrative, a constant telling of stories in this way can lead to frustration. If we are constantly unseen and working under oppressive forces, we are powerless to change our circumstances. This may reflect a passivity that we need to address and can lead to persistent low feelings if we constantly feel like we lack power and recognition.

A constant quest

A journey of many challenges on the way to a larger goal in many ways is a positive narrative. However, if we have many narratives that are quests, we are journeying long and hard and fighting often in order to achieve our goals. We can become worn down by the effort and the distant (or never arriving) reward. Everything is always such a big and sustained effort.

Everlasting confusion of the comedy

If we are leaning toward this narrative in all of our stories, we are really immersed in a state of confusion. We may constantly feel misunderstood and this can cause frustration. Alternatively, we may be continuously deferring happiness, figuring that if people could just understand then... The endless frustration and the lack of happiness in the now are concerns for people who are always telling their stories as comedies.

Endlessly lamenting

Tragedies are not always sad, but they are certainly something that we no longer invest in. When we see the events of our lives as tragedies, we give up on them. The healthy thing is to lay them to rest and move on. However, if we constantly tell our stories as tragedies, we can become 'quitters' and not invest in a situation to make it work out better. And if the tragedies are indeed sad, we would be in a constant state of grief over the circumstances of our lives if this is how we narrated the events.

Perpetual rebirth

Whilst looking internally is often the most empowering thing we can do, if we always look internally we may fall into the trap of thinking we are not enough. That there is something wrong with us or our situations we find ourselves in are always our fault. We may also find that we are focused on changing something that is the wrong focus and so we live with the frustration of never getting anywhere.

Permanently on a journey

The learning journey is such a valuable thing, but if it is our consistent narration, we may find that we allow ourselves to exist in a world where we are always out of our comfort zone and we are always putting up with circumstances that are unfavourable.

HOW CAN LOOKING FOR PATTERNS IN MY NARRATION HELP ME?

Remember that we CHOOSE how we tell our stories. What we are telling is not the truth but a lens through which we are observing or narrating our worlds and the events and facts of our lives. We can choose to tell our stories in seven different ways. It makes sense that we are reflective on how we are telling our stories so we can live our best lives. When we observe deeply the patterns through which we are telling our stories, this can be a wakeup call to change our thinking, to look at our life events through a different lens, and ensure our own agency and our own happiness.

It is healthy for us to be deeply reflective and observant of how we tell our stories over time. We can then be aware of patterns and disrupt those that do not serve us or embrace those that do.

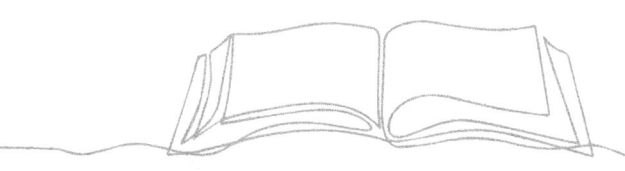

The impact of our emotions

Trevor has an embarrassing problem. He has genital herpes. It is an issue for him. Sometimes it was a small eruption and then it would go away for months, even a year. Other times it will keep erupting and he never seemed clear of the problem.

Trevor had been focusing really hard on his health. He quit drinking and was working out regularly but not too much! He was eating much less meat in his journey toward veganism. He was sleeping better than ever. Yet he experienced another eruption.

Trevor was LIVID.
He felt that all the hard work he had been putting in was for nothing. He shouted, complained, swore at the problem. He had no idea what he needed to do in order to beat this thing.

This was a monster.
Eventually he calmed down. He started to look for more information. He explored the latest studies that linked protein consumption to a flare up. Trevor was starting to see this as a comedy – if he could get to the truth and find out the facts, he would find a resolution.

It is interesting to see the progression of Trevor's attitude and behaviour as he changed his narrative. Initially, when he was overwhelmed by emotion, he could only put his fists up and behave in a pugilistic manner. However, once the initial emotional reaction fell away, Trevor was empowered to find a solution to his problem.

REFRAMING

It pays for us to be aware of how our emotional states affect us and our telling of stories. It pays to be reflective regarding this and be willing to change in order to find solutions to our life conflicts.

Sometimes controlling our emotional states can be difficult. We might use affirmations to help with a general state where we are more in control: 'I am in control of my emotions'. However, once a strong emotion has hold of us, the affirmation becomes less useful.

The first thing we need to do when experiencing strong emotions is to breathe. Use the breathing technique described previously. This will change the physiological responses in the body from stress to relaxation. The body will receive a hit of feel good hormones and you will find that your emotions have had a modification (if not a reversal).

It may be important to find a distractor at this point. Choose an activity that will continue the release of feel good hormones, like exercise or something else that might make you feel good – hugging your children, patting the dog, driving the car.

When your emotions have regulated, revisit the problem and see if you can recognise the narrative you are telling. Then, see if you can reframe the narrative so it serves you to accept your circumstances and potentially find resolution.

HOW CAN OBSERVING MY EMOTIONAL STATE WHEN STORY TELLING HELP ME?

When we recognise our emotions, we can be aware of how they have a physiological effect on our bodies and we can change that. When we observe how our emotions impact how we tell our stories we can be reflective of our emotional states, disrupt them and retell our stories in ways that are more likely to serve us.

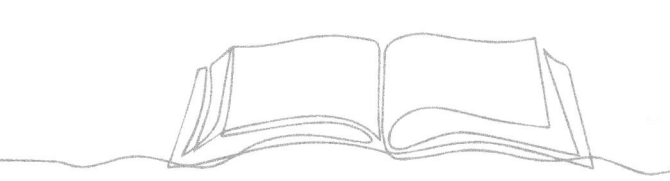

Hitting on the right narrative

It seems to me that the narrative that I tell myself which seems to be the 'right one' is the one that makes me feel the right way when I am journaling the story or visualising it. If it infuses me with positive energy – be that fighting energy, acceptance or some other emotion – so long as it feels right, I know that I am on the right track with narrating this story to myself in this way.

If I have got it wrong, equally, I know.

... contradictory information jars... error jars...
It encourages us to engage in a new way.

- Matthew Syed

When we have the wrong narrative in play it feels uncomfortable; it feels wrong. I know, myself, when I have hit on the narrative that is going to serve me, it feels right. It feels appropriate and I know elementally I am on the right course.

The immersion in your story within the frame of narratives told in the different ways is key. As I reframe my story and think about my narrative told in several different ways, I can feel emotions inside of me – my physical responses to the reframing of the stories – and I know which one is the right one because of the responses I am having.

As Covey says, 'An inner compass will always give us direction,' (p.101). This elemental feeling of rightness and wrongness is innate to us. The only advice I can give to you is to work on that immersion. Fortunately for us, as humans, we have the ability to picture things that aren't real. We can try out all kinds of paths and outcomes before they become reality along the journey of working out which of the narratives will serve us at any given time. Use your imagination to invoke the images and feelings associated with a pathway forward and really feel how you would feel if that were your reality. Allow those feelings to be your guide as to what is the right path for you.

HOW CAN KNOWING I HAVE THE RIGHT NARRATIVE HELP ME?

When we know we have the right narrative because we feel it fundamentally, we can be sure we are on the right path in our lives. We can go forward with confidence and agency.

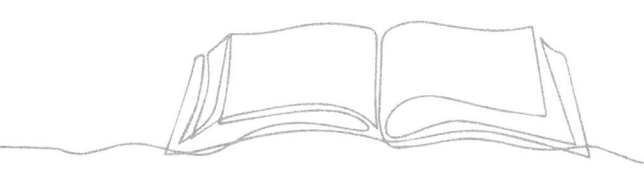

Practice, practice, practice

In order to make this information work for you, in order to be able to apply the narratives to your life and how you narrate stories to yourself, you are going to have to get to know the stories. Be very familiar with the seven narrative types and look for those threads that define them, like the conflict and resolution.

Listen to yourself. Listen to how you tell stories. Listen to others. Observe how others tell stories. Practice.

Repetition is the mother of skill. **- Tony Robbins**

Find the stories in everything and practice identifying which narrative is at play. Listen to newsreaders and hear how they are telling the stories. Read feature articles and examine them for the narrative elements. Watch movies and TV shows. Explore the narratives in adverts. Identify the seven narratives in everything you see and hear.

Sometimes it is easier for someone else to recognise the stories we are telling ourselves than to find them in our own stories. Talk with others about your stories and get their opinion. It takes a lot of practice to be able to self-examine and identify the narratives in our own stories. I trained hard to be able to identify my own narratives. I have revisited the elements of the stories and how they might end and applied those to the stories I am reflecting upon in order to be clear about the plot line present.

Familiarise, apply, practice.

Getting to know the stories, applying your knowledge to the stories around us and doing it over and again is the way forward. This will make it possible for you to recognise the narratives when you use them yourself and give you better recognition of the narrative choices you have so that you can apply the alternatives.

When you are skilled at identifying the narratives in stories, work on considering the alternative ways in which the stories can be presented using as many of the other six plot lines that you can make fit.

And if the narratives are not obvious in the stories you are telling, simply overlay the narrative deliberately. Try as many of the narratives as you can make fit the events. I think that deep inside yourself the narrative is being told according to one of the seven, but you are only being conscious of the events. This is not a problem. Use the tools you have been given in this section of the book to help you move out of habit based thinking and into thinking consciously in terms of the seven narratives.

HOW CAN PRACTICING IDENTIFYING THE NARRATIVES HELP ME?

We need to really know these narratives to be mindfully constructing the stories of our lives. The only way to get better at doing this is to familiarise, apply and practice.

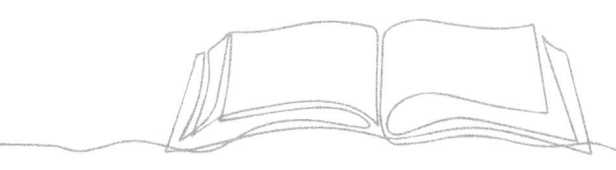

The Seven Stories applied: Teaching the monsters

I was teaching in a low socio-economic high school south of Perth. Teachers would know that when you say 'low socio-economic' you are referring to all of those things that go with it; behaviour being the most prevalent issue for educators in these schools. The kids were tough.

I had a class of year nine students for English. They were naughty, didn't listen, swore, were rude and didn't follow instructions. They didn't do the work. They weren't interested in anything I had to teach them and they were really awful to myself and each other. I started really hating going to the class and they started hating going there too. The more we hated it, the more we hated it.

THEY AREN'T LITTLE MONSTERS!

I was seeing the class as a monster to be overcome. I had pitted myself against the class trying to behaviour-manage them into better behaviours. A 'me against them' mindset. A fight to see who could win. And no one was winning- not me, not those kids. I was so frustrated because nothing I was doing was working. I was becoming ground down by my experience. I was emotional. This narrative wasn't serving me.

NOR IS THIS A TRAGEDY

Buried in my emotions, I grew in my dismay at the class. I felt I had no ability to move things forward. I started to see the whole situation as a tragedy. I was beginning to give up on the class. I was starting to think that if I just put up with it and bide my time, soon enough the year would end and I would not have to put up with them any longer. The amount of times colleagues had bemoaned a class and followed it up with a: 'bring on the end of the year!' It is clearly a theme amongst my peers who have been in a similar situation.

However, giving up on these kids just didn't 'feel right'. How could I feel the conviction of my beliefs if I were to give up on these kids? Pondering that made me feel sad for the students and the loss of potential. And all they were guilty of was being born to a set of circumstances and then had that compounded by being assigned a struggling teacher. I didn't think this story was quite finished. Perhaps I hadn't tried everything.

I AM BORN AGAIN

I did some pretty deep reflecting on this situation. I wrote in my journal, contemplating what was going on. I started to think consciously about how I was telling this story to myself. I started to look for solutions in other places; new pathways forward.

As teachers, we are taught that there are three dynamic areas of teaching where adjustments can be made. These are: the student, the work and the teacher. I was pretty confident in the work. I did not feel I had any power over the students- everything I tried had failed. That left me, as the teacher. I decided that my power was in changing myself.

The other thing I knew was that kids 'work for the teacher'. Particularly in the case of low socioeconomic areas- kids are relationships based. We didn't have a positive relationship. They did not feel liked. I needed to dig deep inside myself and find a way forward. I started to visualise how things would be if I started to show them that I liked them. My body started to fill with positive feelings. I used affirmations such as, 'they are just kids' and 'they deserve more'. This really started to feel right to me. I was sure I was hitting on the right narrative.

I was narrating this story as a rebirth. I was mired in a situation that was displeasing but what I realised was that change has to come from me for things to improve. I was willing to do the work.

And I made a simple change. The first thing I did when I went back into that class was to smile.

The class changed from that day. They smiled back. They started to engage. We all began to get along with each other.

I ended up having the same group through to the end of year ten. They remain, to this day, my favourite class I have ever taught. We really hummed! In fact, we often burst into song. When I think of them my heart warms because of the fond memories of togetherness and the real synergy we found. Once I had chosen to change myself; to make my attitude positive towards being in the class and showed the kids some love and respect, they also changed. The result was wonderful. This narrative truly served me and my students! My willingness to have an open-mindedness to change- a growth mindset- allowed me to look for other ways forward. The approach of *The Seven Stories* was effective in allowing me to take control in this life situation and to find the best way forward from the circumstances of my life.

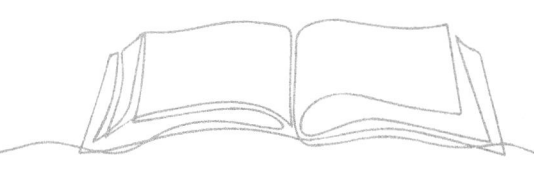

Final Words

It is fair to say that we in the self-help community have a common understanding – readers, writers and thinkers alike – that we tell ourselves stories and we have the capacity to choose our own adventure. And if we have the right tools with which to do this, we will be endowed with the capacity to narrate our stories in the way that best serves us.

We really want to be able to cope with what life dishes up and to be able to find the most appropriate resolution to our situations. In order to do this, we need to be able to recognise the stories we tell ourselves and be upskilled in making other choices. Knowing that there are only seven choices and being familiar with these choices provides us with the information we require. The toolbox in this book provides the strategies to apply this knowledge so we can make our best choices.

We can practice identifying the stories that are told by exploring them in everything around us. Soon you will be finding all of the seven in the unlikeliest of places – songs, fairy stories, magazine articles, adverts – and you will become proficient at identifying the stories you are telling yourself.

If we are having difficulty in identifying our stories, we can simply apply any of the narratives to the events of our lives and choose to tell these stories to ourselves using the seven plotlines with deliberateness. If we find we are so immersed in the emotion of a story that we can't see it any other way, there are tools such as meditation and box breathing that can help us shift out of a stress response and into a relaxation response, giving us the opportunity to see more clearly without the weight of emotion clouding our perception.

Stephen Covey describes humans as having four endowments which give us the opportunity to make proactive choices. These are:

- **Self-awareness:** knowing that we are having experiences and making choices. Being able to see ourselves from the outside.
- **Imagination:** being able to see past what we are experiencing, to other possibilities and times beyond the now.
- **Conscience:** knowing the difference between wrong and right.
- **Independent will:** our ability to act based on our self-awareness and free of all other influences.

(Covey, p.70)

We are indeed self-aware and need to ensure that we are taking the time to step back from our lives, to pull back from the immersion in our life experiences, and to observe what we are going through dispassionately so we can see it for what it is. When we know what our alternatives are for imagining how our lives can be perceived and thus lived out, such as illustrated by the framework of the seven narratives, we can apply those alternatives and imagine substitute pasts, presents and futures. We can imagine the positive and negative consequences of each of these and how we must proceed if we are telling the narrative in that way. Using our imagination further, we can visualise these alternatives and immerse ourselves in the feeling of each alternative.

Our moral compass will kick in and our feelings will tell us which is the right narrative to choose. When we tell ourselves a story, our concern is with one character – its hero. They are the one whose fate we identify with, as we see them gradually developing towards that state of self-realisation which marks the end of the story. When we tell our own stories, we are the hero. If we want our hero – ourselves – to be deserving of the reward in the plot, we need to ensure their (our) moral compass is intact. This guides us to our behaviour and the 'rightness' of the narrative we choose.

We can then apply our independent will to make the choice that best serves us. We can revisit visualisation and apply affirmations to drive ourselves forward into the best future we can possibly have, having made an informed decision about the direction we wish it to take.

Thus, as humans, we can see ourselves from the outside. We can imagine other possibilities for ourselves, perceive which will work for us morally or otherwise. We can decide which stories feel right to us, and we have the opportunity to take our own thinking into account and act on it.

When we are reflective, deeply reflective, about the way in which we tell ourselves stories we can also be aware of the patterns we are exhibiting in this telling. We can explore whether the patterns of our telling are serving us or holding us back and we can make the appropriate changes.

There is plenty of talk 'out there' about telling ourselves stories and making choices about it. What I am offering here is a framework for recognising HOW we are telling ourselves our stories and how we may structure our stories differently. Then we know that we have choices about how we tell our stories and what those choices are. We can see clearly the implications of all of the possibilities and then we can make informed choices.

The Seven Stories We Tell Ourselves framework gives us the opportunity to reframe our narratives, to see things through a different lens, so in the very least we can accept our circumstances. We may also then be able to find a clear pathway forward to find resolution to our problems or issues.

Ultimately it gives us agency, reminds us we have choice and puts us in control of our lives.

Which narrative will you choose?

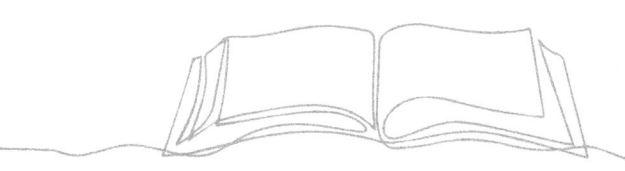

References and Bibliography

Becker, Joshua (2021) "The Stories We Tell Ourselves", in *Becoming Minimialist*, available at https://www.becomingminimalist.com/the-stories-we-tell/ date accessed 20th Jan, 2021

Bennett, Taylor (2018) "How Can Journaling Help Me: Tips for Keeping a Self Care Journal" in *Thriveworks*, available at https://thriveworks.com/blog/journaling-tips-keeping-self-care-journal/#:~:text=Journaling%20is%20an%20incredibly%20beneficial,get%20to%20know%20yourself%20better, date accessed, 22nd Jan, 2021

Bonaiuto M, Mao Y, Roberts S, et al. Optimal Experience and Personal Growth: Flow and the Consolidation of Place Identity. *Front Psychol*. 2016;7:1654. doi:10.3389/fpsyg.2016.01654

Booker, C. (2004). *The seven basic plots: Why we tell stories*. (London: Continuum)

Brown, Brene (2012) *Daring Greatly* (UK: Freedom House)

Christian, Lyn (2021) "Defining Your List of Values and Beliefs", in *Soul Salt,* available at *https://soulsalt.com/list-of-values-and-beliefs/* , date accessed 21st Jan, 2021

Covey, Stephen R. (1989) *The Seven Habits of Highly Effective People: Restoring the Character Ethic* (New York: Simon and Schuster)

Didion, J. (1979) *The white album*

Duhigg, Charles (2012) *The Power of Habit* (New York: Random House)

Hill, Napoleon and Stone, W. Clement (1961) *Success Through a Positive Mental Attitude* (Harper Collins: Sydney)

History.com editors (2011) "Hercules", in *History*, available at https://www.history.com/topics/ancient-history/hercules date accessed 30th Jan, 2020

Jeffers, Susan (1987) *Feel the Fear and Do It Anyway* (New Zealand: Random House)

Jung, C. G. (1980) *The Archetypes and the Collective Unconscious.* (Princeton, N.J.)

Kakutani, Michiko (2005) "The Plot Thins, or are No Stories New?" in *The New York Times*, available at https://www.nytimes.com/2005/04/15/books/the-plot-thins-or-are-no-stories-new.html date accessed 7th Feb, 2021

Mayo Clinic Staff (2020) "Meditation: A Simple, Fast Way to Reduce Stress", in *Mayo Clinic*, available at https://www.mayoclinic.org/tests-procedures/meditation/in-depth/meditation/art-20045858#:~:text=%22Meditation%2C%20which%20is%20the%20practice,disease%20and%20high%20blood%20pressure, date accessed 22nd Jan, 2021

Mind Tools content team (2018) "Using Affirmations: Harnessing Positive Thinking" In *MindTools*, available at https://www.mindtools.com/pages/article/affirmations.htm, date accessed 23rd Jan, 2021

"Monomyth: Hero's Journey Project" in *Berkley Orias*, available at https://orias.berkeley.edu/resources-teachers/monomyth-heros-journey-project, date accessed 20th Jan, 2021

Moore, Catherine (2020) "Positive Daily Affirmations: Is there Science Behind It?" in *Positive Psychology*, available at https://positivepsychology.com/daily-affirmations/, date accessed 23rd Jan, 2021

Parker, Clifton B (2015) "Embracing stress is more important than reducing stress, Stanford psychologist says" in *Stanford News*, https://news.stanford.edu/2015/05/07/stress-embrace-mcgonigal-050715/ date accessed 30th Dec, 2020.

Robbins, Anthony (1991) *Awaken the Giant Within* (New York: Simon and Schuster)

Shapiro, Marc (2000) *J.K. Rowling: The Wizard Behind Harry Potter* (New York: St. Martin's Press)

Shetty, Jay (2020) *Think Like a Monk: Train Your Mind for Peace and Purpose Every Day* (New York: Simon and Schuster)

Stinson, Adrienne (2018) "What is Box Breathing" in *Medical News Today*, available at https://www.medicalnewstoday.com/articles/321805, date accessed 22nd Jan, 2021

Swami, Om (2021) "Stories We tell Ourselves" in *Om Swami*, available at https://os.me/short-stories/the-stories-we-tell-ourselves/, date accessed 20th Jan, 2021.

Syed, Matthew (2015) *Black Box Thinking* (London: John Murray)

"The Picture of Dorian Gray" In *Spark Notes*, https://www.sparknotes.com/lit/doriangray/summary/, date accessed 19th Jan, 2021

Vilhauer, Jannice (2018) "3 Effective Visualisation Techniques to Change Your Life", in *Psychology Today*, available at https://www.psychologytoday.com/au/blog/living-forward/201806/3-effective-visualization-techniques-change-your-life, date accessed 23rd Jan, 2021

Acknowledgements

To my niece, Charli Strickland, for her art work illustrating the seven narratives. You are awesome!

To my niece, Miki Strickland and my gorgeous SiL, Emma, you gave me some super feedback.

To my husband for the lovely cups of coffee. And for finding my typos. Two times over. And for spreading the word of *The Seven Stories*. And my children for understanding I still love them even though I am buried in my office.

To Kate for her professional opinion on the cover art.

To Gillie who gave me some fabulous feedback on my manuscript. You are gold.

To Kagan, you are a constant provocation to new thoughts and ideas. You patiently wait for me to give up my resistance

To all of you who shared your stories with me and allowed their inclusion in the book.

To my FaceBook community who have been supportive all the way.

To Podium Public Speaking for the platform from which to spruik.

Gratitude to the Napoleon Hill foundation for agreeing to allow me to reproduce the story of Ben Cooper. *Naphill.org*

Thanks

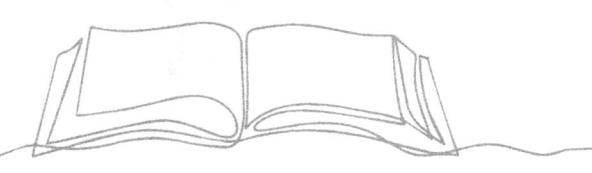

About the Author

Angela Tomlinson lives to add value to every endeavour she pursues and to the lives of each person she meets, which is lived out in her work as a personal development coach. Holding a BA in Comparative Literature and a DipEd, Angela has been an educator for over twenty years. She is an experienced public speaker and is the co-founder of Podium Public Speaking.

The Seven Stories We Tell Ourselves is Angela's first book, but she warns there will be many.

Angela can be found at www.angelatomlinson.net and is available for coaching, workshops and public speaking events.

Where your future begins

www.podiumpublicspeaking.com

CPSIA information can be obtained
at www.ICGtesting.com
Printed in the USA
BVHW072326050721
611166BV00006B/155